DEFEND THE WEST

THE CULTURE OF FREEDOM

Edited by Dr Kevin Donnelly AM

"To fight against untruth and falsehood, to fight against myths, or to fight against an ideology which is hostile to mankind, to fight for our memory, for our memory of what things were like - that is the task of the artist. A people which no longer remembers has lost its history and its soul."

Aleksandr Solzhenitsyn. BBC Panorama program
March 1, 1976

ACKNOWLEDGEMENTS

Whereas a previous anthology I edited titled *Cancel Culture And The Left's Long March* focused on the origins and dangers of cultural-Marxism, rebadged as political correctness and more recently being Woke, this anthology serves a different purpose.

Instead of denigrating, undermining and attacking Western culture and Australia's success as a Western liberal democracy, this anthology celebrates and acknowledges a unique culture, for all its limitations and faults, that well deserves the title *Defend The West: The Culture Of Freedom*.

Firstly, thanks to those whose financial support led to the anthology's publication and thanks to the Page Research Centre for its support in what is a vital contribution to the public debate. Michael Wilkinson Publishing must also be thanked for having the foresight and courage to publish a book that challenges the prevailing cultural-left orthodoxy.

Secondly, the success of any anthology depends on the contribution of the numerous authors involved. It is their knowledge, expertise and ability to communicate that makes my role as editor a less onerous task.

Dr Kevin Donnelly

Published by:
Wilkinson Publishing Pty Ltd
ACN 006 042 173
PO Box 24135
Melbourne, Vic 3001
Ph: 03 9654 5446
www.wilkinsonpublishing.com.au

A catalogue record for this
book is available from the
National Library of Australia

NATIONAL
LIBRARY
OF AUSTRALIA

Title: Defend The West – The Culture of Freedom
ISBN(s): 9781923259102

Design by Spike Creative Pty Ltd
Ph: (03) 9427 9500
spikecreative.com.au

Printed and bound in Australia by Ligare.

CONTENTS

FOREWORD

In the 2023 British Social Attitudes Survey, an annual statistical survey conducted by the National Centre for Social Research, respondents were asked whether they were proud of Britain's history. A decade ago, 86% said they were. In 2023, that had fallen to 64%, a decline of 22 points.

This is an astonishing finding – astonishing that the figure isn't lower. Scarcely a day passes without another blow raining down on Britain's history. A recent nadir was the refusal by the owners of Gunwharf Quays in Portsmouth to allow a statue to be put up honouring the West Africa Squadron, the Royal Navy flotilla that freed about 150,000 slaves. The landowners said the memorial would be out of keeping with the 'welcoming and inclusive' environment it wanted to foster. Meanwhile, Sadiq Khan, the Mayor of London, has unveiled a memorial to the victims of the Transatlantic slave trade at the West India Quay in London's Docklands designed by Khaleb Brooks. "Khaleb's work is a stark reminder of the pain and suffering caused by transatlantic slavery and the role the UK and London played," said the Mayor.

But this wasn't the low point. It never comes. Monitoring these assaults on our national pride is like falling through a collapsing building: every time you think you've reached rock bottom, the floor gives way and you find yourself tumbling through space again. So, Britain's largest teaching resource website recently published guidance on how to make the history curriculum 'anti-racist'. The British Empire, it said, should not be taught as "an equal mix of good and bad". On the contrary, teachers should "present the British Empire as you would other global powers that committed atrocities, e.g. Nazi Germany". I don't suppose they'll linger for long on the West Africa Squadron.

Of course, such self-flagellation has always been a feature of the English intellectual class. In a famous passage in 'England Your England', George Orwell wrote:

> *In left-wing circles it is always felt that there is something slightly disgraceful in being an Englishman and that it is a duty to snigger at every English institution, from horse racing to suet puddings. It is a strange fact, but it is unquestionably true that almost any English intellectual would feel more ashamed of standing to attention during 'God Save the King' than of stealing from a poor box.*

What's new is that this anti-patriotic feeling is no longer confined to intellectuals. It's one thing when "every fruit-juice drinker, nudist, sandal-wearer, sex-maniac, Quaker, 'Nature Cure' quack, pacifist, and feminist in England", to quote Orwell again, is openly contemptuous of our heritage. Quite another when this sentiment goes mainstream. The new manager of the England football team – the Birmingham-born Lee Carsley – refused to sing the national anthem at the beginning of his first game in charge. Can a nation survive when it isn't just a few over-educated radicals who think there's no moral difference between its colonial past and the Holocaust?

I used to take some comfort from the fact that this self-loathing was largely confined to England, with rest of the English-speaking world still committed to upholding the values of the West. I remember spending a year at Harvard in the mid-1980s and being astonished by how patriotic even liberal American college students were. Among the 10 people studying politics at my small Oxford college, opinions ranged from Mosleyite fascism to revolutionary communism. But among the hundreds of people that comprised the Harvard Government Department, the only disagreement was between Rawlsian and Nozickian liberals – two versions of the same American creed. Just as Britain could accommodate a few left-wing intellectuals decrying king and country in the 1940s, so the

Anglosphere could cope with the mother country turning on itself provided the others remained steadfast.

But that's no longer true, obviously. The rot has spread from the head down. At the 2024 Harvard commencement ceremony, over 1,000 students walked out in solidarity with the people of Palestine. As the historian David Starkey recently said when I asked him how much longer he gave Western civilisation, "It's Rome 476, dear boy".

Is he right? As I enter my 60s, I oscillate between hope and despair without much in between. On bad days, I fear for the future of my four children, imaging them being interned in a Chinese re-education camp in Aldershot where they're forced to eke out their days working in a solar panel factory. But on good days I think of all the glorious achievements of our forebears, particularly their resilience in seeing off previous threats to the West, from the 300 Spartans onwards.

The contributors to this book have diagnosed the problem and have some pretty good suggestions about how to address it. It's now up to us to summon the spirit of Sparta 480 BC and say to the hordes massing at our gates, 'You shall not pass.'

Toby Young is the director of the London based Free Speech Union and an associate editor of The Spectator.

INTRODUCTION

Since the dawn of civilisation – actually since neolithic times when prehistoric man first began to settle down, to sow, to plant and to harvest – culture *has sustained and defined us, and it is not by chance that we use the same word when we speak both if cultivating our gardens, and of* cultivating *our minds. Indeed, culture is the true and unique signature of man.* **Pierre Ryckmans.** *The View from the Bridge: Aspects of Culture.*

Pierre Ryckmans, in his 1996 ABC Boyer Lectures, argues culture is one of the most significant features of man. Ryckmans, a sinologist who taught at the Australian National University, also argues that if students are to have any chance of understanding a foreign culture they first must have "a firm grasp" of their own.

While Ryckmans defines culture in terms of "cultivating our minds", it is important to note T.S. Eliot, in *Notes Towards a Definition of Culture*, adopts a much broader definition when referring to culture as the "the way of life of a particular people living together in one place". Included in this way of life are a society's political and legal institutions, its art, music, language, literature, dance, rituals and rites, its approach to education, and most importantly, according to Eliot, its religion. Eliot writes "no culture can appear or develop except in relation to religion". The British philosopher and cultural critic Roger Scruton makes the same point when he writes in *Culture Counts*, "every culture therefore has its root in religion, and from this root the sap of moral knowledge spreads…".

When detailing what constitutes a civilisation's culture, both Ryckmans, Eliot and Scruton suggest cultures are unique, not only geographically and how they originated and evolved over time, but also, more importantly, the way of life they embody, enrich and sustain. A Chinese culture is different to an Islamic culture and a tribal Aboriginal culture is different to a pre-European settlement Māori culture. The Bible and Judaeo-Christianity underpin Western culture, whereas Hinduism is associated with India, Confucianism with China, Islam with the Middle East and Shinto and Buddhism with Japan.

While now condemned as politically incorrect, it is also true that some cultures are more civilised, worthwhile and beneficial compared to others. As argued by Karl Popper in *The Open Society and Its Enemies*, throughout history it is possible to identify those cultures that are tribal and "closed" and those more civilised and "open" where rationality and reason prevail and citizens live free of tyranny and exploitation.

Notwithstanding the prevailing cultural left, Woke ideology championing multiculturalism, otherwise known as diversity and difference, the reality is nations like Australia, New Zealand, the United Kingdom, Ireland, the United States of America and Europe owe their heritage and unique nature to Western culture. While such nations are distinctive and have evolved and changed overtime, especially as a result of migration and the impact of new technologies and global commerce and trade, their origins, institutions, language and way of life share much in common.

As detailed in chapter one, it is impossible to understand or appreciate what makes Western culture unique without acknowledging the impact and on-going debt owed to ancient Greece and Rome and the emergence of Judaeo-Christianity. Paul Morrissey writes, "If we use the analogy of marriage, the West is born from a union between Greece (Rome) and Israel (Jews/Christians). This marriage was not without friction, and required centuries of forging, but its fruitfulness is undeniable".

Whether the concept of democracy, the vital importance of cultivating wisdom, truth and what constitutes the good life and how best to contribute to the common good or its contribution to philosophy, medicine, science, history, politics, literature and the arts there is no denying ancient Greece is one of the foundation stones on which Western culture is built. Philosophers, including Aristotle, Socrates, Plato, Archimedes and Euclid, to name a few, began a conversation that is on-going and still relevant today.

Ancient Rome provides another foundation stone on which Western culture is built. While famous for its engineering feats involving viaducts and sturdy roads linking the empire, of greater importance are the orators and philosophers, including Cicero, Gaius Gracchus, Marcus Aurelius and Tacitus, who addressed perennial questions about how best to structure society and to live a fulfilling life.

Morrissey, when detailing the Rome's contribution to the West refers to Cicero and his belief in what is called natural law, a situation where "true law must conform to nature, and specifically human nature. This law is universal and unchanging, and inscribed in the universe by God, who is reasonable. Law and truth are synonymous".

Judaeo-Christianity is the third foundation stone on which Western culture is built. Morrissey argues both Judaism and Christianity embrace the concept of the one universal God and the belief God's teachings provide moral and spiritual guidance that is true for all people and for all time. Morrissey writes:

> *Thus, Israel and the Christian Church contribute the universalising belief in one God. This belief has untold consequences for the rise of Western culture; a way of worship, a codified morality, and a belief in the inherent dignity of all as created in the image and likeness of the one true God.*

Central to the survival and prosperity of any culture is how each succeeding generation is introduced to and becomes familiar with the patrimony associated with the particular culture into which they are born. In the second chapter, titled 'Liberal Education – An Education for an Open and Free Society' Colin Black details the characteristics of a liberal education, an education essential if a society is to survive, prosper and ensure liberty and freedom for all.

The origins of a liberal education can be traced to ancient Greece and the belief such an education is neither utilitarian nor practical in nature, instead, it is concerned with liberating the mind in the search for wisdom, beauty and truth. While originally centered on the seven liberal arts, over the years the concept of a liberal education has been broadened to include teaching what Matthew Arnold terms "the best that has been thought and said".

Central to a liberal education is initiating each generation into an ever-evolving, cultural patrimony that is underpinned by Western culture's best validated knowledge and artistic achievements. A liberal education, instead of indoctrinating students with Woke mind control and group think, also champions impartiality, rationality and reason. The ideal is one where students are morally grounded, spiritually and emotionally enriched and culturally literate.

Different cultures employ various ways to order society and to decide how power is distributed and maintained. Different cultures also vary in their approach to enforcing the law, some use coercion and violence while others adopt a system ensuring justice, equality and fairness for all.

Augusto Zimmermann in chapter three details the unique way Western culture structures and orders society and how the law is enforced and maintained. Central to Zimmermann's thesis is that it's impossible to fully understand the rule of law without considering its social-political-cultural context. The approach to governance and the law in Western societies like Australia did not happen accidently or arise spontaneously, both are deeply rooted in the nature and evolution of Western culture. Zimmermann writes, "It is from ancient Greece that 'democracy' as a concept was born, from ancient Rome that the written law based on the idea of natural law was developed, and from Christianity that the inherent dignity of the person was boldly proclaimed". Enlightenment thinkers including John Locke and Charles de Montesquieu added to the West's concept of how best to structure and manage society by stressing the importance of concepts like the inherent dignity of the person, the need for a separation of powers and the right all have to a fair trial based on the presumption of innocence.

While often ignored by Woke idealogues, Zimmermann makes the point that the West's legal system is underpinned and informed by Christianity. To suggest otherwise is to raise the spectre of state dominated control, Zimmermann writes, "Excising belief in God leaves us deeply vulnerable to the power of the State. In this situation, there is no mediating structure to generate moral values and, therefore, no counterbalance to the power of the State".

Chapter three stresses the need to distinguish between government through the law and government that abides by the law. One of the defining characteristics of Western culture is that it is a culture of freedom; rulers and governments must accept their power is limited and that what the American 'Declaration of Independence' describes as the God-given right to "Life, Liberty and the pursuit of Happiness" takes precedence.

To fully understand and appreciate the special nature of Western culture it is vital to consider the central importance of Judaeo-Christianity. While all cultures, to a greater or lesser extent, deal with existential questions about the meaning of life, how to find fulfilment, what constitutes right and wrong and what happens after death the Bible offers a unique perspective.

In chapter four Anna Krohn details the work of the Australian academic Margaret Somerville who puts the question: is it possible to decide right from wrong without reference to religion? To put it another way, can a secular society survive and prosper without the moral and ethical compass provided by religious teachings?

Drawing on the writings of Aleksandr Solzhenitsyn, the dissident and Nobel prize winning author who experienced imprisonment in one of Russia's many gulags, Krohn notes that central to Solzhenitsyn's survival is his deeply felt and lived religious experience. To survive one must find solace and meaning in what only religion offers, that is, a deeper and more profound sense of the spiritual and transcendent.

The second figure Krohn refers to is the English philosopher Gertrude Anscombe who made famous the term 'consequentialism'. Instead of accepting the argument the ends justify the means

Anscombe argues decisions must be evaluated in terms of their moral and ethical nature and, most importantly, their consequences.

As detailed in chapter five, notwithstanding there is much to acknowledge and celebrate about Western culture there is the enemy within intent on destroying what is most valuable, beneficial and precious in terms of the on-going debt owed to the West's patrimony. Neo-Marxist inspired cultural-Marxism, more recently rebadged as political correctness and being Woke, now infects the West's institutions and way of life to such a degree that commentators argue Australia, America, the United Kingdom, New Zealand and Europe are facing an existential crisis.

While classical Marxism has always sought power for power's sake based on Lenin's belief "Morality is whatever brings about the success of the proletarian revolution", cultural-Marxism seeks to overturn Western societies by taking the long march through the institutions. As a result of the Frankfurt School being established in the late 1920s and the associated rise of critical theory schools, universities, the church, family, the media and intermediary organisations have been infected with a nihilistic, destructive and barren ideology.

Gender and sexuality, instead of being God given and biologically determined, are social constructs, rationality and reason are condemned as binary, Eurocentric and guilty of white supremacism, the purpose of education is to enforce cultural-left mind control and group think and Judaeo-Christianity is banished from the public square and when deciding government policy.

When analysing why Western cultures are so susceptible to the enemy within chapter six identifies what Roger Scruton describes as oikophobia as one of the key reasons. While most people are conservative in nature, finding satisfaction and fulfilment in family, local community and a sense of national pride, Woke elites enforce a cosmopolitan, global perspective sceptical of those criticised as less educated and xenophobic.

Despite fears about Western culture's demise Gerard Holland, in chapter seven, details why there is cause for optimism and hope.

Globally, the tide is turning as more and more authors, academics, think tanks, media commentators and concerned citizens engage in the culture wars and fight for sanity, common sense and what is best about the West.

Holland applauds the liberating impact of the new digital technologies in providing a dynamic and fertile public space for anti-Woke commentators and academics to engage in the battle of ideas. Examples include Jordan Peterson, Joe Rogan and Heather Heying who use the intellectual dark web as alternative to the Woke mainstream media.

Holland, as evidence the tide is turning, also cites examples like Florida's Governor Ron DeSantis protecting parents' rights to stop their children being indoctrinated with radical gender theory, the closure of the British Tavistock gender clinic and President Trump appointing conservative judges to the Supreme Court.

If culture is upstream of politics, it's also true education is upstream of both, as suggested by a quote attributed to President Abraham Lincoln, "The philosophy of the schoolroom in one generation will be the philosophy of the government in the next".

In chapter eight Diff Crowther argues the global emergence of schools dedicated to a classical/liberal education is evidence many parents and teachers are reacting against the cultural-left's Woke curriculum now infecting schools. Such an education, drawing on ancient Greece and ancient Rome as a well as Catholic theologians including Saint John Henry Newman, centres on Western culture's great books, intellectual rigour and the pursuit of wisdom, beauty and truth.

The growth of schools and tertiary institutions in the Unites States of America, the United Kingdom and parts of Europe as well as the emerging movement in Australia, including Brisbane's Saint John Henry Newman College and Sydney's Campion College, are evidence that in the darkness small fires are being lite.

Anthony Dillon in chapter nine argues the 60/40 vote against establishing an Indigenous Voice to parliament is evidence Woke ideology pushing identity politics and victimhood is not always successful. Central to Dillon's argument, while acknowledging the often-destructive impact of European settlement, is that it's wrong to blame Aboriginal disadvantage on the arrival of the First Fleet in 1788.

Dillon writes, "While I acknowledge the role of British settlement in disrupting Aboriginal people's way of life initially, I do not believe that Western culture is the *cause* of suffering among Aboriginal people *today*". Instead of wasting time, energy and resources blaming the sins of the past as the cause of Aboriginal disadvantage, Dillon argues the focus must be on practical solutions known to work, including solutions directed at improving health, education, welfare and building stronger communities.

While it is natural in a world dominated by soulless, barren and irrational Woke ideology to be pessimistic, chapter ten argues there is cause for optimism. Fiona Mueller, drawing on Edmund Burke's concept of a partnership between those who are living, those who are dead and those yet to be born, writes "It is a constant feature of the human desire not simply to survive, but to thrive".

Rationality, reason and logic, best exemplified by the history of formal speech making and debating that can be traced to ancient Athens, are enduring qualities underpinning Western culture. A healthy dose of scepticism is also a quality characterizing Western culture that helps ameliorate the more extreme, dangerous and irrational elements of cancel-culture.

Whether the Brexit vote calling on the UK to leave the European Union, the on-going popularity of President Donald Trump, the success of centre-right parties in Europe or the vote in Ireland to reaffirm the traditional role of women as mothers and home keepers, there is mounting evidence sanity and reason might yet prevail.

One of the most disturbing examples of Woke indoctrination is the way indigenous history, culture and spirituality are lauded and beyond criticism while Western culture is demonized and condemned as Eurocentric, patriarchal, binary and oppressive. In Australia's national curriculum there are hundreds of references to Aboriginal culture and history based on the belief that Indigenous Australians lived in a pristine Garden of Eden devoid of prejudice and conflict. Such is the degree of infection teachers are told to teach Aboriginal mathematics and science.

Even worse, the school curriculum either ignores, belittles or condemns Western culture and Judaeo-Christianity as irrelevant and guilty of prejudice and hostility towards the 'other'; including people of colour, LGBTIQA+ people, women and anyone else identified as suffering disadvantage and exclusion.

As argued by Anna Krohn in chapter four, once a society turns its back on its cultural memory and inheritance it quickly loses the defining character that ensures cohesion, stability and prosperity and, as a result, division and disunity soon follow. Examples include ethnic no-go zones in London and Paris, the scourge of home-grown terrorism in the United Kingdom and Europe and the climate of disjointedness, anxiety and lack of identity prevailing in Western nations.

The title of this anthology is *Defend The West: The Culture Of Freedom* based on the fact, for all it sins and faults, Western culture is unique in that within itself it provides the ability to recognize and remediate the injustices and wrongs inflicted on others. As argued by Arthur M. Schlesinger Jr in *The Disuniting of America*:

> *There remains, however, a crucial difference between the Western tradition and the others. The crimes of the West have produced their own antidotes. They have provoked great movements to end slavery, to raise the status of women, to abolish torture, to combat racism, to defend freedom of inquiry and expression, to advance personal liberty and human rights.*

It is only Western culture that could produce the *King James Bible*, the 'Magna Carta', the 'Declaration of the Rights of Man and of the Citizen', 'A Vindication of the Rights of Women: with Structures on Political and Moral Subjects', the 'American Declaration of Independence', and the 'Universal Declaration of Human Rights'.

Thankfully, as the following chapters illustrate, not all is gloom and doom. In the darkness there is light as across the Western world the pendulum is swinging back to rationality, reason, common sense, beauty and truth.

Dr Kevin Donnelly, since first warning about the dangers of politically correct language control and group think in the mid-1990s has established himself, in the words of Sky News' Peta Credlin, as "one of Australia's foremost culture war warriors". He is a vocal defender of Western civilisation and Judaeo-Christianity against the destructive and nihilistic impact of neo-Marxist inspired Woke ideology. He writes regularly for the print and digital media, including: The Australian, The Daily Telegraph, The Catholic Weekly, Quadrant, the Australian Spectator and the London based Conservative Woman.

Chapter One

THE ORIGINS AND NATURE OF WESTERN CULTURE

The contemporary West has lost its moorings. For some, especially in elite parts of our culture, this represents the success story of progressivism, whereby a systematic opposition to Western culture has infected institutions of learning and our culture in general. This opposition has many roots, but principally it is Marxist inspired cultural theory that has given rise to an identity politics we now see influencing virtually every sphere of society. The politics of identity reduces truth to power and progress is reduced to inversing the hierarchical pyramid of power in the West. Progress means to move forward, to stand on the heads, and not the shoulders, of the giants of the past. And while progress in knowledge and understanding have been at the heart of Western civilisation, progressivism as an ideology is a poison to the universal ideas and institutions that have made, nourish and underpin Western culture.

Unfortunately, while the West's patrimony is still recognisable, and some skeletons remain of the West's cultural inheritance, most people today live in an uncertain world, lacking meaning, and trying to exercise a freedom without any sense of the true or the good. In the words of Bob Dylan, "Freedom just around the corner for you, but with the truth so far off, what good will it do?".

In this chapter I will look at how Western culture was conceived in a marriage between Greek wisdom (Athens) and Jewish/Christian revelation (Jerusalem). The root of Western culture and its preeminent characteristic was its universalising nature – for the Greeks this involved a pursuit of universal wisdom, the truth of the human person, political ideals, learning, etc. For the Jews (and subsequently Christians), it involved a universal belief in the one true God.

The marriage between Athens and Jerusalem was not without some difficulties, but its fruitfulness was the great culture that is the West. This culture, although born in geographical locations, was never beholden to a particular race or place, contrary to the popular leftist critique of Western civilisation, because of the universal principles that were its motivation. And thus, Western culture has championed universal principles such as human dignity, natural law, human rights, the rule of law, freedom, democracy, etc. These principles have been grounded in and supported by Judaeo-Christian beliefs in revealed religious doctrine and moral teachings. It has also fostered the pursuit of truth resulting in tremendous developments in science.

Western culture is synonymous with universal ideas, and, in many respects, the derision with which the West is often held is due to the attempt to undermine these ideas. Perhaps the most brilliant example of a contemporary critique of this undermining is Douglas Murray's, *The Madness of Crowds: Gender, Race and Identity*. Murray lays out plainly and with numerous examples the toxicity of identity politics and its deleterious effects on rational discourse. This identity movement places limited value on objective truth (which is, as a notion, identified with a Western, white and patriarchal identity), preferring to see everything through a lens of power. The only truth is the hierarchical pyramid that needs inversing. Everything else is oppression. Hence, like so many others, Murray correctly sees parallels with Marxism. However, if an idea is universal, it is true, always and for all people. This claim is almost outrageous today given the prevailing belief each person is entitled to his or her own subjective view of the truth and the belief emotion outweighs rationality and reason.

Ancient Greece is the birthplace of many of the universalising ideas of Western culture. The civilisational contribution of ancient Greece is too great to detail in depth: politics (the republic and democracy), philosophy (the love of wisdom), medicine (Hippocrates and his oath), science (Aristotle), history (Herodotus and Thucydides), literature (Homer, Sophocles and Euripides), education (paideia and the liberal arts), architecture (the glory of Athens), sport, civic life, the military, etc. For our purpose here I will focus on those great Athenian thinkers whose pursuit of truth (the universal) help define the culture of the West.

Near the entrance to the temple to Apollo in Delphi is inscribed the maxim, "Know thyself." This maxim was much discussed by Socrates and has echoed down through the centuries of Western culture. The beginning of wisdom is self-examination. In his *Apology*, Socrates extols his fellow citizens to pursue wisdom and truth and to not let the care of "money and honour and reputation" distract them. There is no higher good than the pursuit of wisdom.

Plato carried forward Socrates' flame, showing that the truth was found in the universal or transcendental ideas that the human mind could comprehend. "Is there not an absolute justice", Plato writes in *Phaedo*, "Assuredly there is. And an absolute beauty and an absolute good? Of course." These ideas are attainable through the light of the human mind, unattached from human senses and desires. And being universal they do not change, they are absolute, and true for all minds. For the Athenian philosophers, truth is not restricted to a particular people, place, or culture, it belongs to all. The West, so to speak, in its universalising ideas, is directed to all points on the compass, though *not* in a colonising sense, but in the sense that all humans are seekers of wisdom and truth, and that this is attainable for all. But not just truth, all the universals, whether it be justice, goodness, or beauty can be sought and attained.

Another universalising theme for the Greeks is their pursuit of the good life, to ask the question, what is it I should do? Ancient Greece's most systematic thinker, Aristotle, answered this question with a profound ethical theory about virtue. Aristotle's ethics are founded on the idea that happiness is the purpose for which all human actions are directed. This insight will be carried forth by great Christian thinkers like Augustine and, more especially, Thomas Aquinas. There are, of course, proximate ends of human actions, such as pleasure, knowledge, and even virtue, that are partly chosen as goods in and of themselves, however, as Aristotle writes, "we choose them also for the sake of happiness, judging that by means of them we shall be happy. Happiness, on the other hand, no one chooses for the sake of these, nor, in general, for anything other than itself".

How can we be happy? In what does happiness consist of? Western philosophy, literature, art, and music are a prolonged meditation and grappling with these questions. Aristotle's great and lasting contribution is his virtue theory of ethics. Virtues are qualities of the soul that are the interior, lasting principles of action. They are learnt from teachers and parents etc., through discipline and explicit teaching, and through repeated good actions they inhere in our soul, become our character. The opposite of virtue is vice. Aristotle was aware that humans are creatures of passion *and* reason, and that it is important to avoid extremes; virtues are the mean between two extreme responses or actions.

In his *Nicomachean Ethics* there are many examples of virtues, such as generosity as the mean (virtue) between the two extremes of senselessly giving away money and to be miserly with one's wealth. Aristotle also bequeathed to Western civilisation the four cardinal virtues: prudence, justice, temperance, and fortitude. The articulation and pursuit of these virtues are a lasting and still relevant contribution of the West. It is an interesting thought exercise to ask who, apart from a sociopath, is against wisdom or prudence, self-control, courage or justice. Surely these are things to strive for and to live for. And yet, the idea that there is some objective good to strive for is seen as quaint or judgemental.

Ancient Rome builds upon and develops the great contribution of the Greeks, but the other founder of Western culture is Israel, and with the coming of Christ, Christianity. This contribution is not philosophical as such, but prophetic and religious. Alone among the ancient world, Israel worships one God, the God of Abraham, Isaac and Jacob. A God that elects a particular people but is always understood and worshipped as the one true God of all creation, of all peoples and all times. Thus, Israel and the Christian Church contribute the universalising belief in one God. This belief has untold consequences for the rise of Western culture: a way of worship, a codified morality, and a belief in the inherent dignity of all as created in the image and likeness of the one true God.

If we use the analogy of marriage, the West is born from a union between Greece (Rome) and Israel (Jews/Christians). This marriage was not without friction, and required centuries of forging, but its fruitfulness is undeniable. "What has Athens to do with Jerusalem?" so asked (rhetorically) the 2nd century theologian, Tertullian. It is a question that has lain at the heart of Western civilisation even before it was first explicitly uttered. Tertullian was in the minority of the Church Fathers in arguing that Greek and Roman wisdom was irrelevant to Christian revelation. St Augustine, perhaps the greatest Christian classicist, argued strongly for the inherent relationship between Judaeo-Christianity (Jerusalem) and Classical culture (Athens). In Book VII of his *Confessions*, Augustine writes of how the philosophy of Plato opened his mind and heart to help him accept the truths of Christianity.

Christianity, it must be said, was a shock to the Roman empire, and the synthesis of the two was not plain sailing. For all its glory, pagan Rome was ripe for a spiritual awakening and Christianity filled this void. As David Bentley Hart has written:

> *Christianity constituted in the age of pagan Rome; the liberation it offered from fatalism, cosmic despair, and the terror of occult agencies; the immense dignity it conferred upon the human person; its subversion of the cruellest aspects of pagan society; its (alas, only partial) demystification of political power; its ability to create moral community where none had existed before; and its elevation of active charity above all other virtues.*

Christopher Dawson, in his work, *Progress and Religion*, argues that the highpoint of the marriage between Athens/Rome and Jerusalem is the Incarnation, when the eternal word, the logos, is made flesh and dwelt amongst us (Jn 1:18). Why? Because it marries the Jewish divinity, the one true God, to the flesh and soul of man, humanity as the highpoint of Greco-Roman world. Christopher Dawson quotes early Christian writers such as Eusebius who writes about man as the artist, the builder of cities, the scientist, the philosopher, man as a God upon Earth, the dear child of the divine word. And St Gregory of Nyssa speaks about the mixture of the eternal and the material that is found in human nature and in a certain sense all of creation is touched by the divine. Dawson notes that the early Church took the "spoils of the Egyptians", the great learning of the classic civilisations, to forge a Western culture, that with ebbs and flows, much light and some darkness, would come to dominate the known world and bequest an extraordinary array of ideas and institutions of lasting relevance. To mention but a few, a legal and political system underpinned by Judaeo-Christianity, the concept of a liberal education and the subsequent establishment of schools and universities, and much of the West's literature, music and art.

In what follows I will address some of the fruits of Western culture and its universalising nature: the natural law, freedom of conscience/religion, and science. Natural law was conceived in Greece but it's historical influence is the result of Rome that assimilated the philosophy of the Greeks with the political reality of the Empire. Around 55BC, Cicero, in his Republic, wrote famously of the natural law:

> True law is right reason in agreement with nature, universal, consistent, everlasting, whose nature is to advocate duty by prescription and to deter wrongdoing by prohibition. Its prescriptions and prohibitions are obeyed by good men, but evil men disobey them. It is forbidden by God to alter this law, nor is it permissible to repeal any part of it, and it is impossible to abolish the whole of it. Neither the Senate nor the people can absolve us from obeying this law, and we do not need to look outside ourselves for an expender or interpreter of this law. There will not be one law and Rome and another at Athens or different laws now and in the future. There is now and will be forever one law, valid for all people's and all times. And there will be one master and ruler for all of us – God, who is the author of this law, its

promulgator, and its enforcing judge. Whoever does not obey this
law is trying to escape himself and to deny his nature as a human
being. By this very fact he will suffer the greatest penalties, even if
he should somehow escape conventional punishments.

Notice here the perennial characteristic of the natural law, and
an acceptance of an 'unknown' God. Cicero stresses that true law
must conform to nature, and specifically human nature. This law is
universal and unchanging, and inscribed in the universe by God, who
is reasonable. Law and truth are synonymous. The natural law for Israel
is inseparable from the divine law of the decalogue, and Christianity
will bring the natural and divine law into a great synthesis, exemplified
in the high Middle Ages by Thomas Aquinas's magisterial ethical
teaching. Fundamental to Aquinas's approach was the following: a
philosophical anthropology, indebted to Aristotle, which examines the
nature of human persons and their choices and motivations; a theory
of practical reason by which moral principles are naturally known
(natural law) and confirmed by faith (divine revelation); a psychology
of human action centred on the virtues, both natural and infused/
theological (faith, hope, and love); and a theology of grace, that makes
attainable the happiness sought by Aristotle in the true end of the
human person, the beatific vision. It should not go uncommented, that
Aquinas's synthesis of Aristotle with Christian morality is one of the
greatest examples of the marriage between Athens and Jerusalem.

Jacques Maritain, the notable Catholic philosopher of the twentieth
century, demonstrated clearly the link between classical and Christian
theories of the natural law and the modern pursuit of human rights.
As one of the architects of the universal declaration of human rights,
drawn up in the wake of the horrors of World War II, Maritain
understood that modernity could agree on some universal rights even
if it couldn't agree about their roots or justification. He saw that unless
there was a return to Christian and classical roots, these human rights
would be on shaky ground – and as the abuse of 'rights' language
becomes more and more common, Maritain has proved to be right. The

only true justification for human rights is the natural law classically defined.

I turn now to a second fruit of Western culture, religious freedom, which I will use as synonymous with freedom of conscience. Freedom of religion is an outgrowing of the inherent dignity of the human person, and one finds its origins in ancient Greece and Rome, where different religions and ideas were tolerated (up to a point). And while the modern notion of religious freedom is associated with the Enlightenment and the end of the so-called wars of religion, the roots of this freedom are more deep-seated in Western culture.

As the historian, Robert Louis Wilken has demonstrated, religious freedom rests on a simple truth: "religious faith is an inward disposition of the mind and heart and for that reason cannot be coerced by external force". Tertullian of Carthage was the first to explicitly state this truth in the early third century, "It is only just and a privilege inherent in human nature that every person should be able to worship according to his own convictions; the religious practice of one person neither harms nor helps another. It is not part of religion to coerce religious practice, for it is by choice not coercion that we should be led to religion".

Wilken argues that Christianity, married to the ideas of classical thinkers, led to the growth of the idea of religious freedom and conscience. And this argument rests on three themes: "first, that religious belief is an inner conviction accountable to God alone and resistant to compulsion; second, that conscience is a form of spiritual knowledge that carries an obligation to act; third, that human society is governed by two powers". As Christ states, "Render to Caeser the things that are Caeser's, and to God, the things that are God's" (Matt 22:22). This truth, more clearly lived out in some epochs than others, is central in the development of freedom.

The development of science, though not restricted to Western culture in the history of the world, flourished in Western culture from the beginning. This development has arguably two main causes. First, the Hebrew scripture begins in Genesis with an account of creation that makes two very important claims. God created the universe *and* the universe (or the natural world) is not God. This means, that unlike a lot of primitive religions, and even the beliefs of some classical pagans, nature is not worthy of worship and is under the dominion of humanity.

It is difficult to do natural science on a 'divine' nature. This second claim of dominion is also crucial in the development of science, but also in any area where humanity has tamed the creation for its benefit, whether it be farming, or energy, mining, etc. This biblical belief is based on an ordered dominion, in union with God, where the human person is a co-creator with God in his work. In fact, science for the religious believer is in no way contradictory. This beautiful prayer from the renowned twentieth century astrophysicist and politician Enrico Medi demonstrates this:

> O you mysterious galaxies... I see you, I calculate you, I understand you, I study you and I discover you, I penetrate you and I gather you. From you I take light and make it knowledge, I take movement and make it wisdom, I take sparkling colours and make them poetry; I take you stars in my hands and, trembling in the oneness of my being, I raise you above yourselves and offer you in prayer to the Creator, that through me alone you stars can worship.

The second main reason why science has flourished in the West is the impact of Athenian philosophers. Their pursuit of truth led naturally to a contemplation of the world around them. This is especially true of Aristotle, who is quite rightly called the father of natural science. As the philosopher of common sense, he trusted the human senses as a conduit to true knowledge and in studying things around him could arrive at deeper and eternal truths (metaphysics). His natural science, sometimes called natural philosophy, led him to discuss causation, motion, and forms. But the Greeks were also famous for their mathematics, the two most famous being Archimedes and Euclid.

There are two great myths when the development of science in the West is discussed. The first myth is that science was born in classical antiquity, died with the rise of Christianity, and was reborn and thrives in the Enlightenment. The second great myth simply says that science was born in the Enlightenment. These myths exist due to the great separation between faith and reason, religion and science, that begin in the Enlightenment and has mostly grown wider ever since. However, like most myths, they rely on a fabricated truth. In his book *God's Philosophers: How the Medieval World Laid the Foundations of Modern Science*, James Hannam expertly describes how the Christian intellectuals of the Middle Ages were truly pioneers of scientific knowledge.

Take, for example, the early thirteenth century Dominican friar, Albert the Great. After a study of the liberal arts (grammar, rhetoric, dialectics, arithmetic, geometry, astronomy and music), he developed a love for the natural sciences. He writes, "For it is (the task) of natural science not simply to accept what we are told but to inquire into the causes of natural things". Pope Benedict XVI wrote of Albert that he shows us that there is no opposition between faith and science, though his "study of the natural sciences and progress in knowledge of the micro and macrocosm, discovering the laws proper to the subject, since all this contributes to fostering thirst for and love of God".

As James Hannan argues, fourteenth century thinkers noticed that Aristotle's natural science has some serious holes, especially in their breakthrough in combining mathematics and physics in a way not done before. One such thinker, Thomas Bradwardine, stated that, "Mathematics is the revealer of every genuine truth... whoever then has the effrontery to pursue physics while neglecting mathematics should know from the start that he will never make his entry through the portals of wisdom". And so, the Middle Ages, rather than a break in the development of science in the West, was a key steppingstone to the scientific revolution ushered in at the time of the Enlightenment. This revolution has indeed produced marvels beyond measure, although like all revolutions its extremes, especially in the ideologies of scientism and scientific materialism are to be regretted (an argument for another day!).

This chapter has argued that Western culture is a universalizing culture, especially founded on the pursuit of truth and wisdom and the belief in the one true God; the idea that there are some things that are true, always and everywhere, about the human condition. However, as is obvious, the fragility of Western civilisation is being laid bare by its inability and unwillingness to pass on these truths. Education is riven with subjectivism and relativism, filled with identity politics and discourses of power, and has broken with wisdom, truth and belief in the one God.

In a recent response to a comment by Elon Musk that freedom of speech is under threat in some Western nations, the former footballer and now public commentator, Craig Foster, tweeted the following, "Truth is subjective. Which is why misinformation and disinformation is so corrosive. They undermine shared understandings and create divisions between groups who cannot even discuss an issue on the same basis, let alone agree, or agree to disagree". Here in this simple tweet, one sees that the enemies of Western universalism (Truth is subjective) still rely on Western universalism (misinformation is corrosive – is it true or not?). This was a point often repeated by the philosopher Roger Scruton who critiqued the various critics of Western culture for their "absolutism" in rejecting Western universal ideas. Scruton was one of the most eloquent defenders of Western culture and so it's apt to give him the last word:

> The universalist vision is the legacy to us of Western culture, and the reason why we should conserve that culture and pass its great teachings to the young. Western culture is our highest moral resource, in a world that has come through to modernity. It contains the knowledge of what to feel, in a world where feeling is in constant danger of losing its way.

Dr Paul Morrissey is president of Campion College, Australia's first Liberal Arts College. He has had a career teaching theology and the humanities at university and high school. He completed his

Licentiate in Sacred Theology at the Lateran University in Rome and his Doctorate at the Catholic Institute in Sydney. He has published widely in Theology, the philosophy of education, religious freedom and various cultural issues.

Chapter Two

LIBERAL EDUCATION – AN EDUCATION FOR AN OPEN AND FREE SOCIETY

A liberal education is difficult to define but can perhaps more helpfully be thought of in terms of what it is not. Whatever else it is, it is not solely a preparation for a specialised occupation requiring a high level of practical skills. In other words, it is not a form of professional or vocational training, of the kind that, e.g., airline pilots or nuclear physicists, must undergo, or the artisan practitioners of the traditional trades, such as electricians or construction workers, gain through their apprenticeships.

Nor is it a politically motivated upbringing for the young, a comprehensive and determined indoctrination that has as its aim the formation of future citizens who will play their committed part in a particular type of society, be it a 21st century secular progressive social democracy now fashionable in the English-Speaking West, with its own holy trinity of Diversity, Equity and Inclusion, along with social limitations on what views may be expressed in public, or the more autocratic or theocratic regimes seen in the majority of member states of the United Nations where, more commonly, unquestioning submission and mass conformity of thought and practice are among the required outcomes.

In terms of the contemporary malaise, it is clearly not an education primarily committed to the formation of "wokelings", people who are forever scouring their world for what they see as disadvantaged groups whom they can sacralise as victims. These young zealots, after the manner of the extreme early Calvinists or Cromwell's Puritans, are following what we might charitably see as a form of 'hyper-Christianity', but one without any possibility of transcendence, forgiveness and redemption.

Again, it is not a programme devoted to contemporary ideas of 'well-being', with mental health as the goal of education. This is the self-esteem movement in schools, where the Holy Grail is the untrammelled happiness of every young person, be that the intellectual happiness of Socrates on his never-ending quest for truth, or the sensual happiness of a pig gluttonously gorging at the trough, a distinction rarely raised by its advocates. There is also the danger that too much self-preoccupation may develop into a form of narcissism, even if we convince ourselves that our concern is not with ourselves, but with the 'victims' we seek to protect. The contemporary young person's goddess Taylor Swift in one of her 2022 songs includes the cynical but insightful lines, "Did you hear my covert narcissism I disguise as altruism? Like some kind of Congressman?".

To flesh out more positively what we mean by a liberal education, it may assist if we look into the classical culture associated with Western civilisation from which it emerged, along with the etymology of the words themselves. The word liberal is derived from the Latin verb *liberare*, which means 'to set free'. Hence the Latin term for a slave who has been set free is *libertus*. A liberal education in classical Greece was thus seen as an education appropriate for free men. It was not to be constrained by considerations related to function or practicalities, but was seen as a desirable activity in its own right.

Moreover, the association of freedom with a liberal education also gives rise to the idea that such an education liberates the mind, that is, it helps to free it from error so that persons educated in this way are more likely to see things as they really are, and not be led down alleyways where everything is, in one novelist's words, "a muddle". In E. M. Foster's *A Room with a View* (1908) an elderly father reflects upon how best to advise his son George:

> *Take an old man's word; there's nothing worse than a muddle*
> *in all the world. It is easy to face Death and Fate, and the things*
> *that sound so dreadful. It is on my muddles that I look back with*

horror – on the things that I might have avoided. We can help one
another but little. I used to think I could teach young people the
whole of life, but I know better now, and all my teaching of George
has come down to this: beware of muddle.

In ancient times a classical liberal education was centred on the
seven liberal arts, the Trivium (Grammar, Logic and Rhetoric) and
the Quadrivium (Geometry, Arithmetic, Astronomy and Music). It
was, however, not until the nineteenth century, if the Oxford English
Dictionary is to be our guide, that the notion of 'educated' came to be
associated with the all-round development of a person, intellectually,
morally and spiritually. The great Public Schools of England and
their transplants to Australia took this very seriously. The Victorians
emphasised 'Godliness and Good Learning', while the writer Graham
McInnes, speaking of his schooling at the Presbyterian Scotch College
in Melbourne in the 1920s, recorded in his memoir that he soon
learned there that "good examination results were the eye of the
needle through which even the bulkiest camel might one day enter
the Kingdom of Heaven".

The Victorians also kept faith with the Roman maxim *mens sana*
in corpore sano – a healthy mind in a healthy body – and a strong
belief in the good effect of games on character development, 'Muscular
Christianity', was embraced wholeheartedly in schools throughout the
then British Empire.

In the second half of the 20th century, phrases like 'realms of
meaning', 'ways of knowing', and 'modes of awareness' began to be
used to describe the development of the rational mind through a liberal
curriculum which would embrace the different ways in which we come
to know and understand our world and ourselves and, in E. M. Foster's
term, lessen the likelihood of our being in a muddle, or simply getting
things wrong.

Philip Phenix, a faculty member at Teachers College, Columbia
University from 1954 – 1981, published his influential work *Realms*
of Meaning: A Philosophy of the Curriculum for General Education

in 1964. His six realms – symbolics, empirics, aesthetics, synnoetics, ethics and synoptics – can be traced in part to the Trivium and Quadrivium of the Ancients, and in his words:

> … may be regarded as comprising the basic competencies that general education should develop in every person. A complete person should be skilled in the use of speech, symbol and gesture, factually well informed, capable of creating and appreciating objects of aesthetic significance, endowed with a rich and disciplined life in relation to self and others, able to make wise decisions and to judge between right and wrong, and possessed of an integral outlook. These are the aims of general education for the development of whole persons.

A curriculum could then be constructed which ensured that the disciplines it contained reflected the totality of the realms of meaning. Synnoetics, e.g., would be covered by such subjects as philosophy, psychology, literature and religion. Perhaps some of these, like philosophy and psychology, might be better left for the post-secondary stage, when students would have a sufficient grounding in other disciplines as well as adequate life experience, to make their study more meaningful.

However, the Phenix model was soon to be under attack from a new quarter. Seven years later, an educational sociologist at the London Institute of Education, Michael F.D. Young, brought out his influential critique of the traditional curriculum *Knowledge and Control* (1971). He spoke there of the "knowledge of the powerful" and argued that "the curriculum always expresses the interests of those wanting to maintain their power". Young's writings were to become increasingly influential in curriculum debate and, for the early neo-Marxists making education the locus of their long march through the institutions, the runs were soon on the board, while arguments for a traditional liberal education in academia were seen as politically unsound if not reactionary.

Among last century's most prominent and prolific advocates of the intrinsic worth of a liberal education, were those colleagues and students who were disciples of Richard Peters, Professor of the Philosophy of Education at the University of London in the 1960s and 1970s, some of whom took his approach back to their home countries, including Australia. Let me give you a flavour of Peters' idea of how he sees a liberally educated person, by quoting a paragraph from the chapter 'Education and Seeing What Is There' in his 1959 book *Authority, Responsibility and Education*, which began as a series of B.B.C. Third Programme talks:

> *An educated person is one who has some kind of understanding. He does not, as it were, just suck up what he sees; he makes something of it in the light of the principles which he brings to it. He fits things into a framework. And he does not just interpret what is before him narrowly. When confronted with a car, for instance, he not only has some understanding of how it works. He is sensitive to its aesthetic proportions, to its history, and to its potentiality for human good and ill. He sees it as a problem for town-planners as well as a fascinating machine. In brief, an educated person is one who has some depth and breadth of understanding. He can appreciate what is there in many dimensions because of what he brings to it.*

"What he brings to it" underlines that, as with most worthwhile things in life, sustained effort and patience over time bring their reward. A grounding in the several disciplines which allow us to interpret experience in a way that demonstrates both depth and breadth of perception and understanding, requires an intellectual maturity achieved over many years of application. Psychologists have long taught that perception is an active and not a passive process. We assimilate what we experience to what we have already learned, and our existing knowledge and understanding accommodate to this new encounter.

Consider, for example, the complex skill of the oenophile, the sommelier or the professional wine-taster. When they are presented with a glass, they see this not as an opportunity to quench their thirst or enjoy a mild euphoria after quickly quaffing the contents. Their educated palette, their sensitivity to the colour of the wine, and their discriminating olfactory powers, mean that there is a myriad of information for them to process as they view, breathe and take their first sip. They will bring many years of mentoring by other masters of the craft to their task, as they reverentially gauge the colour, the bouquet and the complexity of the taste as it gently moves around the mouth.

Their knowledge of winemaking will bring speculation as to whether new or traditional techniques have been employed in the wine's production. Perhaps they will recognise with satisfaction or surprise the *terroir* where the vines were planted, when this was done and by whom. As they sample the fruits of the vineyard, they may picture the region, its people and its way of life, as it has changed over the decades. If they are commercially minded, they may reflect upon the popularity of such wines, their scarcity and the demand for them throughout the world at the present time.

The more romantic may reflect upon the age-old role of a shared bottle as a social lubricant, a part of human fellowship, while at the same time being aware of more contemporary concerns regarding over-indulgence and its negative consequences for health and society. They may also recall that Jesus's first recorded miracle was the turning of water into wine at the wedding at Cana and that, for Christians, God's Son lives today at every Mass in the chalice proffered to the faithful.

In short, the richness of the experience of the wine-taster is boundless. It is almost as if there is an eternity of experience to be savoured in every sip from the glass. The philosopher Roger Scruton has explored such pleasures in his delightful encomium *I Drink Therefore I am: A Philosopher's Guide to Wine* where the world of the classically educated polymath meets that of the refined oenophile.

The idea of education as an initiation into forms of thought and ways of knowing brings to mind the rituals which are associated with the initiation *rites de passage* of young members of societies both past and present. Investing any activity with tasteful ritual, which has a long history, is one way in which we underline for those not yet able to articulate or understand, the great significance of what is taking place.

Lessons and lectures may not be ceremonies of initiation, but their effectiveness is increased if they share something of their magical tone.

This is why we should cling to the vestiges of educational rituals which are still in practice, albeit in decline. We recognise that the pomp and ceremony of our courts of justice, and our more traditional places of worship, communicate in this way a sense of mystery and transcendence and, without needing to put it into words, the deep value to the culture of what is transpiring therein. In the defence forces, saluting the rank and not the holder of the rank, emphasises the hierarchical order and the need for respect and obedience, which create the morale and discipline necessary in a fighting unit.

Long-ingrained habits of classroom etiquette, tastefully organised assemblies, prize-giving ceremonies which celebrate high achievement, a dress code for both pupils and teachers – these are worth preserving for their role in marking out for children that schools are special places even if at the time they do not understand why. We can think of them as fall-out shelters from the worst features of contemporary life on the outside and to which the young are ready prey – emotional incontinence, social media, parochialism, conformity to Woke ideology, preference for short-term gratification, and the relentless pursuit of things transient and material.

Similarly in universities, there is still a place for ritual, and this is evident even in these more prosaic times when informality is more likely to be favoured. Graduation ceremonies, formal dinners in hall, collegiate life and, as in in North America, the wish to join fraternities and other arcane societies with their cryptic language and eccentric practices, communicate the impression that students are involved in something significant even if this is not openly articulated.

Related to ritual is the role of stories and myths as a way of holding onto and handing down our beliefs, traditions and values to the next generation. This is one of the oldest forms of education we have – Greek and Roman mythology, Old Norse legends, the parables of Jesus of Nazareth, the fables of Aesop, the fairy tales of the Brothers Grimm. We warm to their narrative power and our imaginations are arrested by it, just as we are stimulated by the unfamiliar language and their content and, more readily perhaps, but without realising it fully, incorporate their timeless insights into the human condition into our way of looking at ourselves and the world.

If we are not given guided access at an early age to our cultural inheritance, in Matthew Arnold's sense of "the best that has been thought and said", then our lives are the poorer. Mark Dooley, literary executor of the late Sir Roger Scruton, summarised the latter's position thus:

In denying students access to their history; in dumbing down art, music, literature, and even the sacred liturgy; and in celebrating obscenity over beauty, you detach people from their past, their home, and the transcendental dimension of the human experience. You make them strangers to themselves, to the soul, and the soil.

A wretched feeling of *anomie* or placelessness, what we often call alienation, engenders a thirst for a place we know and feel confident to call home, and where we will be confirmed in our membership. This place has the potential to enchant us, embracing as it does the shared heritage into which we have, in no small part through our liberal classical education, been initiated. We are the proud guardians of the culture we have inherited; our literature, music, art, architecture, political and legal institutions, and our religious rites, form the building blocks of our common home, and are the source of what Scruton calls our *oikophilia*, a Greek word which means love of home.

There is a moving scene in Alan Bennett's 2004 play *The History Boys* when Hector the eccentric schoolmaster explains his vocation:

Pass the parcel. That's sometimes all you can do. Take it, feel it and pass it on. Not for me, not for you, but for someone, somewhere, one day. Pass it on, boys. That's the game I want you to learn. Pass it on.

Then there are those delightful advertisements for Patek Philippe watches, where a young boy looks admiringly at his father's wrist. The caption reads, "You never actually own a Patek Philippe watch.

You merely look after it for the next generation". Both Hector and the advertising copywriter capture with admirable simplicity the essence of the conservative concept of education and, in particular, the body of knowledge – D. H. Lawrence called it "the holy ground between teacher and taught"– to which both teacher and pupil owe allegiance, and which we have, as Edmund Burke reminded us, a duty to safeguard as our obligation is not only to the living, but also to those yet to come, and to those who have gone before.

It is, however, salutary to remind ourselves that the spirit of the times for over a century has not been sympathetic to those committed to the value of a subject-centred, traditional education.

> *The word education comes from the root e from ex, out, and duco,*
> *I lead. It means a leading out. To me education is a leading out*
> *of what is already there in the pupil's soul. To Miss Mackay it is*
> *a putting in of something that is not there, and that is not what*
> *I call education. I call it intrusion, from the Latin root prefix in*
> *meaning in and the stem trudo, I thrust.*

The above is from Muriel Spark's 1961 novel *The Prime of Miss Jean Brodie*, where the Edinburgh schoolteacher of the same name finds herself in conflict with her conservative headmistress. The words encapsulate amusingly a pedagogical debate which has been going on for over two centuries, since Rousseau first published his education tract *Emile* in 1762. The opening sentence is an early example of what Scruton has called the culture of repudiation, in which a culture's fundamental cherished values and practices are dismissed forthright, "God makes all things good; man meddles with them and they become evil."

Rousseau's writings were to influence over a century later the educational theory of John Dewey and his disciples in the United States, where a progressive pedagogy was embraced, especially methods which sought to draw out ideas from the child, rather than have them explicitly taught or, in Miss Brodie's contemptuous term, "thrust" on the pupil. This was not some more contemporary form of Socratic questioning where the teacher's aim was, by careful questioning, to elicit the concepts which they were seeking to have articulated, but a child-centred approach where, it was fancifully imagined, complex ideas would blossom like flowers in the kindergarten in the sun of the teacher's smile.

Over the years, there has also been a debate as to whether education owes its derivation to that other Latin verb *educare*, which means to bring up or rear, and has, according to the Oxford English Dictionary, been used in the context of the training of animals or even the propagation of plants, perhaps what Miss Brodie had in mind when she saw traditional pedagogy as a form of intrusion. She would have been at one with Paolo Freire's criticism in his *Pedagogy of the Oppressed* of what he called the "banking model of education", where the teacher merely makes deposits into the students' minds which they passively accept.

An emphasis on the child, rather than on the teacher, gradually found its way into Government reports in the United Kingdom and in Australia as the cultural revolution of the 1960s made its presence felt; the catch cry, 'I am no longer the sage on the stage; I am the guide by the side' was proclaimed with a note of triumph; the well-tried and tested phonic and phonemic awareness approach to reading instruction gave way in favour of the whole word 'look and say' method; desks in rows were rearranged into small group tables in the classroom where children faced one another rather than the teacher.

While a strong case can be advanced for the value of a liberal education, one whose foundations lie back in the mists of classical time, there are a number of reasons why we are unlikely to see a resurgence of this tradition on any widespread scale at this time in Australia. There have long been undergraduate colleges dedicated to the liberal arts in the United States, many of them well established and highly prized. 'Greats' (a rigorous study of Classical History, Philosophy and Languages), and P.P.E. (Philosophy, Politics and Economics) at Oxford, are demanding and highly competitive with a long history and they carry great prestige.

To be fair, each has its own focus on a body of knowledge and does not have the breadth of a genuinely liberal arts programme. However, it is only relatively recently that a few schools and colleges in this country have seen the liberal arts and a classical education as their 'core business' and promoted such a programme vigorously. Campion College outside Sydney is one of very few pioneers in the tertiary sector, while the Australian Classical Education Society lists little over a handful of schools on its website at this stage.

It is understandable that those bearing the cost will wish to be clear as to the value of their investment. It is much easier to convince those who are considering funding such ventures, be they governments utilising tax-payer money, parents willing to pay tuition fees, or philanthropists attracted by the idea of founding new institutions of learning, if the benefits can be clearly shown in terms of end results. However, the idea of education as an end in itself as an process which has its own intrinsic value and is not to be judged in purely instrumental terms, is not something that sits easily in a relatively young society where there is an understandably pragmatic emphasis on making things happen so that the country prospers, and the accepted markers of success are inevitably economic.

Another common objection relates to relevance, which has been a bugbear of education for almost a century. Children and young adults, and their parents, wonder how what is going on in classrooms and lecture theatres is related to the 'real world', by which they usually mean the employment market. While this cry may carry less weight now that people generally accept that young people today may in the future be engaged in work which we cannot yet imagine, what G. H. Bantock called "The Parochialism of the Present", still carries force.

We must also accept that a traditional liberal education is not for everyone. The prospect of committing oneself to the demanding study of arcane texts containing complex and unfamiliar ideas, requires a dispassionate focus on content, analysis, and synthesis on the part of the student who, at the same time, is expected to have faith in the value of the enterprise even if it seems at the time to have no clear endpoint.

This is perhaps even more so at present, when the very existence of the Western canon is questioned by those of a neo-Marxist bent who view much that was valued by previous generations as evidence of white supremacy and subjugation of 'the other', be they downtrodden members of the proletariat or people of other than pale skin colour.

There is also the consideration that the teaching methodology ideally suited to liberal education, derived as it is from the ancient Socratic method, involves constructive and open interaction among fellow students and with their teachers, when informed views culled from close study can be expressed and discussed constructively. It is a sad feature of campus life in Australia and elsewhere that such freedom of speech is under threat and that scholars and faculty must constantly monitor what they say lest they be accused of racism, hate speech, heteronormativity or other such present-day shibboleths.

In spite of so many obstacles and counter-currents, those who continue to be convinced of the worth of a classical liberal education should not be too downcast. There are 'little fires' being lit for us by Edmund Burke's "little platoons", in Australia and elsewhere. As Richard Peters has reminded us, perhaps we can take heart from George Eliot's heroine of her 1871 novel *Middlemarch*, Dorothea Brooke, of whom the author wrote at the end of her novel:

> *But the effect of her being on those around her was incalculably diffusive; for the growing good of the world is partly dependent on unhistoric acts; and that things are not so ill with you and me as they might have been, is half owing to the number of those who lived faithfully a hidden life, and rest in unvisited tombs.*

Colin Black OAM grew up in Scotland and is a graduate of the universities of Edinburgh and Glasgow. After working in the secondary and tertiary sectors in the United Kingdom, he emigrated to Australia at the age of thirty to take up a lectureship in Education at what is now Curtin University. He then held senior positions at Scotch College, Melbourne, including that of Vice Principal.

Colin was Headmaster of Camberwell Grammar School for seventeen years and was awarded the Centenary Medal and Medal of the Order of Australia for services to education. He has been a Klingenstein Visiting Fellow at Columbia University New York. After retirement Colin lived and worked in London for some years before returning permanently to Melbourne in 2023.

Chapter Three

THE RULE OF LAW AS A CULTURE OF FREEDOM

This Chapter provides a broad account of the social-political-cultural elements leading to the realisation of the rule of law. In doing so, it contends it is unfeasible to properly comprehend and appreciate the obstacles facing the realisation of the rule of law if confined simply to the observation of the legal-institutional phenomena. Rather, a proper understanding of obstacles facing the realisation of the rule of law can only be achieved if a more ambitious interdisciplinary analysis is undertaken, addressing the legal, institutional, political and cultural issues pertaining any particular society. It is also argued those societies most successful in adopting a rule of law guaranteeing freedom, justice and liberty are indebted to Western culture.

It is from ancient Greece that 'democracy' as a concept was born, from ancient Rome that the written law based on the idea of natural law was developed, and from Christianity that the inherent dignity of the person was boldly proclaimed. As the heir to these important traditions, Magna Carta championed fundamental rights and Enlightenment thinkers including John Locke and Charles de Montesquieu fashioned classical liberalism as a foundation for an open and free society based on the protection of these basic rights of the individual.

Consequently, this chapter provides an interdisciplinary analysis of the rule of law, considering whether or not the realisation of this important ideal of legality may be intrinsically dependent on the broader cultural characteristics of society as much as on its formal legal system, by examining the interactions between the two. Since the rule of law, indeed, is consistently dependent upon a socio-politico-cultural milieu, the intention is hereby to demonstrate how this ideal of legality is as much a socio-political-cultural achievement as it is a legal-institutional one, as it cannot be disassociated from the moral traditions of society.

The rule of law, therefore, does very poorly in cultures where the protection of fundamental rights is not regarded as a primary expectation that people have of their government. As noted by the British lawyer and academic Sir Ivor Jennings KBE QC FBA, "If it is believed that the individual finds his greatest happiness, or best develops his soul, in a strong and powerful State, and that government implies... the unity of the [community] behind a wise and beneficent leader, the rule of law is a pernicious doctrine".

Although the meaning of the rule of law is always open to debate, there is general agreement it is essentially concerned with protecting the citizens from unpredictable and arbitrary interference with their vital interests. Under a rule-of-law regime, all public authorities, including judges and politicians, must be subjected to basic rules and principles that are thought to be socially desirable on various grounds associated with liberty and justice.

In this sense, an underlying theme in legal philosophy is that the rule of law provides at least part of the solution to the problem of tyranny, here understood as the existence of any abusive external control over the life, liberty, and property of the citizen. Thus, a community acquires the protection of the rule of law if every person is legally protected from all forms of arbitrary violence, and if laws exist that are established to avoid a Hobbesian state of "war of every man against every man".

However, once laws are created to regulate private coercion and violence, the government itself can become the primary source of arbitrary control and violence. This leads to laws being extended to the regulation of governmental action, so that law ceases to be only a rule among citizens and it also becomes a rule among rulers.

In this sense, this ideal of legality involves a delimitation of the power of the State. The rule of law effectively requires that such power must be exercised according to clear, stable, and general rules of law. These rules must be promulgated by the elected legislator in advance and enforced by an independent and impartial judiciary. By forcing civil authorities to follow legal rules and procedures, the rule of law operates to reduce the possibility of government being able to excessively coerce, obstruct, or otherwise unreasonably interfere with the life, liberty, and property of the citizen. Of course, this naturally requires an appropriate separation of powers. The primary characteristic of separation of powers is its assertion of a division of governmental agencies into three different branches: legislature, executive and judiciary. This doctrine is deemed an essential element to ensure abuse of power is prevented.

Historically, the phrase 'rule of law' was primarily used with reference to a belief in the existence of laws – natural or divine – possessing higher authority than the law promulgated by the State, thus, imposing limits on its power. The idea can be traced to Aristotle, who argued it is far better for the law to rule all the citizens, so even those in charge of the government are also subjected to the law. First coined by Aristotle, this ideal of legality was meticulously elaborated by St Thomas Aquinas, who stated once a government is established, such government "must be so arranged that opportunity to tyrannize be removed".

At the same time, its power should be so tempered that it cannot easily fall into tyranny. For Aquinas, we are bound to obey government in so far as this is required by the order of justice. If government commands what is unjust, we are not bound to obey it except perhaps in order to avoid danger. Hence, if the government commands what is objectively unjust, the people are not bound to obey such an unjust command. These Christian doctrines of resistance to tyranny were present in the Middle Ages at least a century before Aquinas.

One of the central elements for the realisation of the rule of law is the general conviction that separating the power of the State is a *sine qua non* condition of every legal system that hopes to combine organisational efficiency and the greatest possible exercise of personal freedom. This separation of powers promotes freedom by setting up more accountability via the competitive interdependence within the separated branches of government. The idea rests upon the view that whenever the power of the State is concentrated in the hands of a person or a group of persons, the risk of arbitrariness naturally increases.

This idea of separation of powers is a unique feature of Western culture. Because our forefathers understood the basic aspects of human nature, they tailored a government suited to our rightful place in God's creative order. Human government is necessary because our evil inclinations toward sin must be kept in check by laws and a government capable of enforcing such laws. Thus, government protects us from our sinful nature. But our forefathers also grappled with the problem of protecting citizens from the sinful inclinations of those in authority.

By broadly distributing power and responsibility, the possibility of abuse of power because of our fallen nature must be minimised. The result of their efforts is our system of checks and balances among the branches of government. Each branch wields specific powers that prevent concentration of power (which is always inimical of liberty) and authority from falling into the hands of a select few.

In a rule-of-law system, the basic rights of the citizen are protected by an independent judiciary endowed with the authority to invalidate legislation on grounds of unconstitutionality, if necessary. Paramount to this model of limited governance is the separation of the branches of government, especially the judiciary. Accordingly, a truly independent judiciary will be empowered to compel government to respect the law, thus protecting the citizens in their enjoyment of fundamental human rights and freedoms.

Of course, even if an independent judiciary might serve as a protector of the rule of law, ensuring that nobody, not even the legislator, violate laws with impunity, such independence by itself does not necessarily guarantee impartial adjudication. Even if constitutionally secured, judicial independence does not necessarily deliver the impartial enforcement of laws, which is one of the things we hope to gain from the rule of law. Independence without strict impartiality can turn the judiciary unto a law in and of itself.

Furthermore, the rule of law is contrary to unelected judges dictating policies by means of judicial activism. Needless to say, judges who adhere to judicial activism are much less inclined to respect legal rules. One such activist judge, Lionel Murphy, an Australian politician who served as Attorney-General in the Whitlam Government, and then sitting on the High Court from 1975 until his death in 1986, deemed precedent "a doctrine eminently suitable for a nation overwhelmingly populated by sheep". Activist judges such as him violate their own sworn allegiance to upholding the law faithfully. They treat judicial work as an act of uncontrolled personal will.

The realisation of the rule of law is not merely a matter of legal-institutional design. In fact, its realisation depends on an interconnected cluster of social/cultural values that can be pursued in a variety of legal-institutional ways. The rule of law, therefore, is a meta-legal ideal. It is an ideal of legality concerning what the laws ought to be. For the rule of law to become a reality, good laws are not enough. A culture of freedom is also required.

In this sense, the answer to the puzzle of how the law can limit the power of the State is that it does not – attitudes about law provide the limits. What gives real life to the rule of law lies in the social/cultural environment, which is constantly at work on the law – destroying here, renewing there, invigorating here, deadening there. Hence, even if good laws are enacted, another and more difficult task is to develop a culture of freedom whereby governments are not entitled to do as it sees fit.

This being so, the rule of law requires the virtue of a populace that desires to enjoy its benefits. If people do not expect such benefits, the rule of law is soon corrupted and replaced by the rule of will. The United Kingdom used to provide a good example as to how the rule of law depends as much on the efforts of a community as on legal-institutional design. Although this country traditionally lacks institutional mechanisms of checks and balances, and even a written constitution, the UK is historically recognised as having achieved more of the rule of law than the majority of its former colonies, some of which enacted 'good constitutions' but may be missing the tacit social approval required to keep these aspirational legal documents alive.

Unfortunately, in our contemporary society the meta-legal elements for the realisation of the rule of law have been considerably overturned by statist ideologies that take no account of the traditional social values upon which this ideal of legality was founded. Excising belief in God leaves us deeply vulnerable to the power of the State. In this situation, there is no mediating structure to generate moral values and, therefore, no counterbalance to the power of the State. Accordingly, statism provides a prime example of society's willingness to deny God and place absolute sovereignty in the hands of the State.

This mistake, which results from a deliberate disregard of God as our ultimate lawmaker offers no salvation except through the hope that the State will perfect us and our environment. Today, some utopian socialists advocate global government as the ultimate political and economic solution to advance humanity's evolution. If they prevail in their attempt to establish a 'new world order' via the complete abandonment of God's moral law, we may well experience the coming of the Anti-Christ (See the book of Revelation!).

When a government does not acknowledge its subjection to the law, power rests not on legal rules and principles but on the sovereign power of the State. As a consequence, the rule of law is gradually replaced by government by law. In this context, those who exercise the power of the State will not subject themselves to the limits of legality but place themselves above the law. They may exercise power *per leges* (by law) but never *sub leges* (under the law). Thus, law is transformed into an instrument for repression or at least top-down direction of subjects, and nothing more. And when this occurs, citizens are subject to the arbitrariness of 'laws' being used as a mere vehicle (and at times useful camouflage) for the exercise of unrestrained power.

Feminist jurisprudence, for instance, which relies on, and overlaps with, Marxist ideology, tend to disregard the rule of law as a manifestation of hegemonic power. Feminist legal theorists thus associate the condition of women in our society as a result of patriarchy that is supported by the rule of law. Likewise, critical legal theorists equally manifest their opposition to the rule of law. One of the most noticeable themes within critical legal theory is the idea that the rule of law, in all its postulation for neutrality and impartiality, provides an ideological mask, or justification, for the exploitation of certain marginalised groups.

Critical theorists, therefore, aspire to subvert the legal system by turning law into a tool of power for political gain. Accordingly, laws become no more than ideological weapons used to beat political opponents into submission. This phenomenon is intrinsically associated with the rise of lawfare. For example, some people in Australia have been found at the receiving end of expensive legal action for merely holding conservative views that are no longer accepted by the illiberal ruling classes. The excessive cost of litigation can of course easily result in the denial of justice, which in itself is a form of punishment and a further denial of the rule of law.

As can be seen, not everyone agrees with this important ideal of legality. Of course, this simply demonstrates that the rule of law is not an ideal universally shared by everyone. This basically confirms that, indeed, the realisation of the rule of law depends on a socio-politico-cultural milieu. Ultimately, its realisation is about citizens appreciating what this ideal of legality can achieve, namely legal protection against arbitrary government and the enjoyment of fundamental rights and freedoms.

Without the effective protection by law of fundamental rights and freedoms, a country may be governed through law but it cannot call itself having the rule of law. The success at sustaining arbitrariness by maintaining a façade of legality arises out of a legalistic approach that shrouds exercises of power which might violate even the most basic rights of the citizen.

Because the rule of law stands in frontal opposition to executive orders which express the temporary will of the government, democratic governments are necessarily bound to exercise their power according to clear, stable, and general rules of law, which must therefore be approved by the elected representatives in parliament and receive proper public scrutiny.

Unfortunately, the Australian legal profession has generally accepted the use of emergency powers by the executive government, thus enabling authorities to issue executive orders that impose heavy fines and imprisonment for non-compliance with certain arbitrary measures. Even the principle of legality is no longer regarded as important by some elements within the judicial elite, at least insofar as the government can allege that an emergency justifies the enactment of measures that profoundly affect the enjoyment of our fundamental rights and freedoms.

In this sense, it might be quite important to consider the role of the legal profession in the legitimisation of oppressive regimes. The example of Germany in the 1930s provides a good case study. Embedded in the legalistic dogma that law is law regardless of its substantive nature, many German lawyers became defenceless against laws of arbitrary or criminal content. These lawyers identified the validity of law only with its source as opposed to its moral merits. By claiming, on grounds of social cohesion, that it is critical to always obey the law, German judges sacrificed the ideal of justice to the legal command of the State, by asking only what was legal and not if the law was also just.

Naturally, the problem of extreme injustice can only be dealt with coherently if we adopt a concept of law that incorporates some basic morality as a limiting criterion. Accordingly, the German legal profession in the 1930s supported the use of emergency powers that facilitated the ultimate denial of ethics and metaphysics in conceptualisations of the law, which eventually resulted in a lack of legal basis for lawful resistance against the Nazi regime.

There is no doubt in my mind that Australia would be able to learn from this dreadful episode of German history. Paradoxically, the ruling political class in Australia has managed to undermine the rule of law through legalistic means. Instead of openly violating the formal legal order, the rule of law has been seriously compromised by the insulation of the ruling classes from any scrutiny and a functioning system of checks and balances, and separation of powers.

Of course, the success of authoritarian endeavours requires popular acquiescence. Convincing the populace of any *emergency* leads to less resistance and more political space in which to expand the powers of the State. To avoid concern for human rights violations, the rulings classes in Australia have learned about the need to manipulate public perceptions so as to win support of what normally would be rejected as unlawful.

For instance, if the ruling classes can convince (manipulate) the masses that a serious 'health emergency' exists (as occurred during the Covid-19 pandemic), then the former faces much less resistance to continue expanding their arbitrary power via the draconian exercise of legislative power. The average citizen then becomes more prone to cede even their most basic rights in exchange for safety and protection. The legal-institutional structures which have well served to protect the individual from external oppression – the *sine qua non* of the rule of law – are weakened and undermined in the process.

The ideal of legality known as the rule of law is associated with a classical liberal tradition of constitutionalism which declares the priority of the individual over the State. Accordingly, the value of the rule of law was hailed by Western jurists as the bedrock of every truly constitutional government, and hence of personal freedom. Since the rule of law must be interpreted in the light of this classical scheme of constitutional governance, the power of the State must be subordinated to enduring legal principles that no governing authority is authorised to abrogate. This tradition, a tradition grounded in Western culture, which declares the priority of the individual over the State, laid the basis for modern constitutionalism and its protection of individual rights and liberties.

In this sense, the rule of law is traditionally recognised as the bedrock of every constitutional government, and hence of personal liberty. Once it is recognised that the conduct of government is constitutionally prescribed, the preservation of fundamental human rights becomes essential to sustain this legal-institutional framework as firmly entrenched in the form of constitutional government which the constitution explicitly ordains. Under this tradition of legality, to be under the law presupposes the existence of laws serving as an effective check on arbitrary power. Without the effective protection of fundamental rights, a country may be governed by laws but it cannot call itself having the rule of law.

Constitutional government – government under the rule of law – requires an appropriate separation of powers. Accordingly, the original drafters of the *Australian Constitution* aspired to achieve the ideal of constitutional government. This foundational document must be always interpreted in a manner that promotes its purposes, values, and principles. In drafting the *Constitution*, the Australian Framers thus sought to design an instrument of government intended to distribute and limit the powers of the State. This distribution and limitation upon the powers of the State was intentionally chosen because of the view that unrestrained power is always inimical to freedom.

At this point someone may assume that the best way to protect fundamental rights is through a judicially enforceable bill of rights. But this is debatable since the interpretation of abstract legal provisions may become indistinguishable from the moral and ideological tendencies of unelected judges. In fact, the experience gathered from 'western democracies' reveal that the premise of judicial protection of fundamental rights via an abstract declaration of rights is rather illusory.

A judicially enforceable declaration of rights confers on unelected judges the power to determine the whole hierarchy of rights. One may argue that this could undermine the realisation of the rule of law, in the sense that interpretation of such abstract provisions can become indistinguishable from the moral and ideological tendencies of judges. This may result in the usurpation of legislative function by an unelected judiciary, as every decision of enacting such documents is also a decision to remove important issues from the agenda of the elected branches of government.

This is why it is possible to argue that the traditional understanding of the judicial function does not sit altogether comfortably with the enforcement of a constitutionally entrenched bill of rights. For example, enforcing a bill of rights may undermine political rights by putting beyond revision other than through the unelected judicial elite what the citizens may have managed to obtain via the democratic process. As such, even when a law is enacted with considerable support of the citizens, this might be challenged and struck down because the citizens' view of what rights one should have does not accord with the judges' own personal views.

To give an example, from 1995 to 2000 anti-partial-birth abortion laws were passed by the elected legislative of thirty U.S. states, generally by overwhelming margins. And yet, in 2000, in the case of *Stenberg v Carhart*, the Supreme Court repealed those laws and declared that any legislation which outlaws "partial-birth" abortion somehow violates the due process clause to be found in the Fifth Amendment of the American Bill of Rights. In writing for the majority, Justice Breyer stated, "We conclude [that the law banning partial-birth abortions violates the Constitution] for two independent reasons. First, the law lacks any exception for the preservation of the… health of the mother. Second, it imposes undue burden on a woman's ability to choose". For those who might not know what that Court deemed a "constitutional right" partial-birth abortion is a gruesome procedure in which babies as old as nine months of gestation are killed by sucking out their brains soon before birth is completed.

Now consider the example of Australia. Of course, our country does not have a federal bill of rights. And yet, abortion on demand became a right on account of two controversial judicial rulings. In 1969, Justice Manhennit of the Victorian Supreme Court held the validity of performing an abortion in order to protect the "physical or mental health of the mother". Two years later, in 1971, Justice Levine in the New South Wales District Court extended the concept by considering abortion equally valid on economic or social grounds. The term health was loosely defined to include all factors – physical, emotional, psychological, familial, and the woman's age.

These decisions of unelected and unaccountable judges, as well as the application of principles of precedent, legalised abortion on demand in Australia. The examples above indicate that any appeal to abstract rights, despite the superficial attraction they normally attract, may in actual fact become a major factor in *depriving* human beings of their most fundamental rights, especially the right to life.

If Australian judges were able to do such appalling things without a bill of rights, imagine then what they might be able to achieve once such abstract declarations are introduced in our legal system. This is why, on balance, any abstract declaration of rights may diminish rather than enhance the legal protection to inalienable rights to life, liberty and property.

Those who believe that an abstract declaration of rights might better protect fundamental rights should consider the examples of China, Cuba and Sudan – all of them countries were basic human rights are grossly violated. These countries have all enacted impressive bills of rights. Even the Soviet Union under Stalin's tyrannical rule was in possession of an impressive bill of rights.

But the enactment of abstract human-rights legislation is not necessarily inconsistent with the rule of law. These documents might be useful in situations where the laws enacted by the State are grossly violating the basic rights of the citizen. Of course, depending on social context entrenching a bill of rights may offer the educational advantage of impressing upon the public mind the value of individual rights and freedoms, thus making them part of a political creed which the population will defend to ensure the fundamental rights of the citizen. In any other situation, and for the reasons above explained, a bill of rights may be quite prejudicial for democracy and the realisation of the rule of law.

The ideal of legality known as the rule of law encompasses traditional Western ideas about liberty and justice and, more generally, requirements of fairness in the relations between governors and governed. The rule of law, therefore, is a meta-legal doctrine concerning what the laws ought to be. As such, the realisation of the rule of law depends as much on a society's culture and way of life as of the law, and on their interactions. This premise rests on an understanding that law is always subject to correlation by standards of truth and justice.

Because the origins of the rule of law are historically and geographically determined, it is always important to consider that the rule of law can only subsist where there is a proper culture of freedom which places a high value on the legal protection of fundamental human rights. In the absence of this perception, a sophisticated rights-based constitution may be drafted but this, in and of itself, will not ensure that these constitutional rights will be necessarily respected, especially by the governing authorities. These rights may in actual practice be not worth the paper on which they are written.

The rule of law depends for its successful realisation on an interconnected cluster of beliefs and values that can be pursued in a variety of legal-institutional ways. The fact that the rule of law has often thrived best where it was least designed indicates that what gives real life to this ideal of legality lies in its social-cultural-political environment. Because the rule of law cannot be disassociated from the moral values and traditions of society, this ideal of legality does poorly in societies such as communist China where freedom and more individual rights are not the primary expectation that people have, even if there is a good legal-institutional framework based on the formal promises of separation of powers and protection of fundamental human rights.

In a rule-of-law environment, therefore, the primary goal of government is the preservation of fundamental human rights, and such government never possesses a reason to remove these basic rights of the individual, or what the American Declaration famously refers to as the God-given "unalienable rights" to "Life, Liberty and the pursuit of Happiness". Accordingly, the realisation of the rule of law rests upon an absence of arbitrary coercion that can only be achieved through the virtue of a populace that will enjoy its benefits. Otherwise, the rule of law becomes an impracticable and even undesirable ideal, and society will quickly relapse into a state of arbitrary tyranny. This helps understand the failure of so many societies, especially those dominated by fascist and communist ideologies, to effectively resist arbitrary attempts by the State over the life, liberty, and property of the citizen.

Clearly, the rule of law is not just about a legal recipe for detailed institutional design. Instead, the rule of law is primarily a meta-legal ideal of legality that, as such, requires a socio-politico-cultural milieu based on a broader appreciation for personal freedom and human dignity. In sum, the realisation of the rule of law is as much a socio-political-cultural achievement as it is a legal-institutional one. Of course, one of the strengths of Western culture is precisely that it best provides the type of socio-politico-cultural milieu so necessary for the realisation of the rule of law.

Augusto Zimmermann (PhD, LLB cum laude, LLB (Hons), CIArb, DipEd). Augusto is Professor and Head of Law at Sheridan Institute of Higher Education in Western Australia, having been a former WA Law Reform Commissioner (2012-2017) as well as former Associate Dean (Research) and Postgraduate Research Director at Murdoch University's School of Law. Professor Zimmermann founded and presides over the Western Australian Legal Theory Association (WALTA), served as Vice-President of the Australasian Society of Legal Philosophy (ASLP) and is the Editor-in-Chief of the Western Australian Jurist law journal.

The author of numerous academic articles and books, he has received multiple awards for academic excellence, including the 2012 Vice Chancellor's Award for Excellence in Research and the 2013 Law Lecturer of the Year Award from the Murdoch Student Law Society (MSLS), in recognition of the outstanding level of teaching provided to the students at Murdoch Law School. Finally, Professor Zimmermann has been included, together with only twelve other Australian academics and policy experts, in 'Policy Experts' – the Heritage Foundation's directory for locating knowledgeable authorities and leading policy institutes actively involved in a broad range of public policy issues, both in the United States and worldwide.

Chapter Four

CHRISTIAN WITNESS: LIVING MEMORY OF HUMAN DIGNITY AND WHY RELIGION MATTERS

At the turn of the millennium before the global unsettling of the pandemic, the now Professor Emerita, Margaret Somerville, published a book which brought fluency to the fractured ethical situation of Western secular societies.

Her book titled *The Ethical Canary: Science, Society and the Human Spirit* aims to re-imagine ethical imperatives and limits in the intersection between human dignity and science, technology and healthcare.

Margaret Somerville an Australian legal scholar, ethicist and something of a public philosopher, envisages, along with disturbing trends in modern healthcare, that she serves as an "ethical canary". What she means by being the titular "canary" is that certain people or events can raise important ethical concerns which serve as early warning signals, signs that the "societal air" has become toxic and potentially lethal in some important cultural or spiritual way. Here she adapts a metaphor from early mining history where caged canaries served as harbingers of dangerous underground gases, they being living-and-dying air quality monitors.

At the time of her book's publication, Somerville explained that she was attempting a "secular sacred" paradigm for societies that had lost a shared ethical "story" which once derived from and rested in a common religious foundation.

Professor Somerville explained at a seminar on her book held at Indiana University in 2004 that, "In the past, we found that story mainly through organized religion, even if, as individuals, we weren't particularly religious".

In *The Ethical Canary* she poses the question, "Is it possible, in a secular society, without using religion as a basis, to come to a societal consensus that some things are inherently wrong?".

The Ethical Canary invites its readers through narrative, symbolism and imagination to a type of shared intuitive metaphysical universe which does not rely on a particular religious faith for appeal. Somerville's vigilant "ethical canary" perches alongside the book's suggested "ethical tools" such as interdisciplinary conversation, respectful public engagement and some core principles including civility, honesty, reasonableness, a regard for the common good and other virtues.

The Ethical Canary Somerville hoped would 'sing' into existence a shared and new public conscience which would question and halt unbridled scientist reductionism, self-interest and the financial forces which drive certain destructive practices and technologies. There are many instances of this ranging from the highly monetized business of reproductive technologies to the use of so-called gender affirming hormones.

These foundational values she admitted did not spring out of an individualistic projection or from a neutral "view from nowhere", subjective ethos. Such values arise from a transcendent view of human life and spirit centred on the 'mystery' and the need for openness and faith as she writes

> ... we also need a sense of something beyond ourselves and of the metaphysical (again, I hasten to point out that does not mean that we have to believe in the supernatural) to guide our ethical progress into the future.

Professor Somerville's presence and proposal, instead of being doctrinaire, is a liberally conversational and convivial one. Despite this hospitable style, her fluency and her eminent academic career, she discovered that her voice was often unwelcome. She acknowledged, in an on-line interview with James K.A Smith and published in the *Comment* magazine, that because of her public opposition to same-sex marriage, euthanasia, and various widespread practices in reproductive technology (she does not mention her own Catholic adherence) that she endured attempts to block or cancel her academic voice and advancement. In the same interview she was asked about her hopeful approach to public ethical discourse, "You feel as though there's probably always something enduring there that you could reactivate in the language that might wake people up to remember, or something like that?".

It seems that Margaret Somerville was not to be accepted or forgiven in some secular quarters for importing into her ethical position even her more diplomatic and user-friendly echoes of the Judaeo-Christian idea of natural law, especially as this frames convictions about human life, sexuality and dignity. No "ethical canaries" are welcome on the backs of ideological sacred cows!

Despite the hostility of the Woke secular opinion arbiters, this chapter proposes that as sectional identity politics works to shut down authentic ethical and social discussion and spiritual capital more 'ethical canaries' are needed.

We need more courageous and imaginative people such as Professor Somerville to remind us our civilisation's existence relies on the synthesis between classical reason, cultural excellence and the revealed Judaeo-Christian theological insights that has been hard wrought over more than two thousand years. The most outstanding and enduring harbingers of this historical and cultural genius are individual human persons who build up traditions and communities around them. They are not only cogent and compelling in their ideas, but they are also movingly authentic in their lives and faith.

The belief in the beauty and goodness of created being, the preciousness of humanity and the human person, the quality of mercy, the real moral and spiritual freedom of human vocation are not memes fabricated in an ivory tower, some spin-doctor's fancy or bureaucratic necessity. They represent that which is best in Western culture's patrimony, even if this comes at great cost to the "canary".

The fragile legacy of Western civilisation in its ethical, humane and cultural foundations is engraved into society as a type of living memory or metaphysics as Professor Somerville hints.

Christians believe that this legacy has come about through the mysterious presence and work of Divine Providence. This bears fruit in the spiritual nobility, intelligence, charity and creativity of historical men and women, many of them saints, who have responded to this grace and are formed by their encounter with the person of the God-man Jesus Christ.

Joseph Ratzinger as Pope Benedict XVI writes in his first encyclical *Deus Caritas Est*, "Being Christian is not the result of an ethical choice or a lofty idea, but the encounter with an event, a person, which gives life a new horizon and a decisive direction".

Far from dismissing these good and even spiritually noble people from ethical discussion, the need is to argue with Joseph Ratzinger that religious faith and specifically Christian faith should not be consigned to history nor to the periphery of our deepest cultural concerns. As Cardinal Ratzinger in 'Interreligious Dialogue and Jewish-Christian Relations' (*Communio* 25 (1998) p. 31) he writes:

> … *It is necessary to experience (religious faith) from within, and indeed, it is only such experience, which is inevitably particular and tied to a definite historical starting-point, (that) can lead the way to mutual understanding.*

This chapter will highlight the thought and example of just two giants of the 20th century who stand as exceptionally important though sometimes prickly ethical canaries (to use Margaret Somerville's vivid term) reminding us not to forget our metaphysical standing or its source in Divine Wisdom.

The two figures discussed will help illustrate how Christian imagination and ethical thinking is personalist and crucial to a civilisation which aims to build a common good around the universals of human dignity, reason, life and creativity.

These two figures also exemplify not only thinkers but disciples who as Ratzinger suggests, formed their witness by living within the mind and the demanding pilgrimage of a sacramental Christian life with its Biblical/mystical language and imagery.

The first of these witnesses is a powerful literary man who converted from a type of civic Marxist-atheism to Russian Orthodoxy and suffered under the machinery of Soviet repression, Aleksandr Solzhenitsyn. The other witness is the brilliant and edgy intellectual woman who combined her outstanding philosophical contributions with a life of outspoken and often uncomfortable Catholic commitment and witness, Elizabeth Anscombe.

In the final decades of the Cold War (1947-1991) one of the world's most commanding voices in defence of freedom, conscience and human dignity was the Nobel Prize winner, novelist and Soviet exile and dissident Aleksandr Solzhenitsyn (1918-2008).

Solzhenitsyn's major works, especially his *Gulag Archipelago* (1973-8), *One Day in the Life of Ivan Denisovich* (1961), *The Oak and the Calf* (1961) and the monumental historical cycle *The Red Wheel* are rightly seen as literary and cultural master pieces which at the same time exposed and contributed to the downfall of the murderous communist tyranny of the Soviet Union in 1989.

These works take the form of narrative history and sometimes in the form of novel or poem. All Solzhenitsyn's work is formed out of existential patchworks woven together by the author's commanding literary voice and, importantly, through his memory of experiences, conversations and insights.

Solzhenitsyn's thick notion of memory included not only memories (as we usually understand them) but also a universal higher intuition that provides the author (and his readers) with a bedrock from which to resist the enforced forgetting of the Judaeo-Christian foundations of both Eastern and Western civilisations.

The Russian dissident often likened this catastrophic loss of memory, which included the "forgetting of God", to a type of societal amnesia which was bolstered by the effects of moral corruption, cultural disintegration and the more sinister mechanics of anti-human ideology associated with fascism and communism.

University of Dublin lecturer Brendan Purcell in *The History of Communism in Europe, vol 1,* 2010 observes in an insightful article titled *Alexander Solzhenitsyn's Overcoming Personal, Political and Historical Amnesia…*:

> *Solzhenitsyn's medium was the narrative restoration of memory, what Plato called anamnesis, where what's being remembered are the core elements of human existence which had been deliberately suppressed.*

The notion of *anamnesis* in this Russian Christian sense is not simply Platonic involving memories of a pre-existent or mythical existence. It is rather an adapted notion, which Cardinal Joseph Ratzinger explains is resonant of the Biblical imperative to heed and attend to conscience in remembering. He explains in *On Conscience: Two Essays*:

> *This anamnesis of the origin, which results from the godlike constitution of our being is not a conceptually articulated knowing, a store of retrievable contents. It is so to speak an inner sense, a capacity to recall, so that the one whom it addresses, if he is not turned in on himself, hears its echo from within.*

It is significant that many of Solzhenitsyn's works are structured as memoirs, observations from life which rely upon the disciplined exercise of the author's memory. While he was a labour camp prisoner he deliberately exercised and rehearsed his faculty of memory, not only to store facts, but as a means of survival and resistance to the cruel and anonymising conditions which he endured.

He writes of finding hope through the severe deprivations in the labour camps by writing poetry onto the rare bars of soap or committing to memory conversations and texts he would later use in his works.

Andrew Zwerneman, in defence of historical thinking, writes in *Solzhenitsyn on Memory: Remember the Forgotten Man*, "No one in the modern age understood memory as well as Aleksandr Solzhenitsyn. More than any other exemplar of modern remembrance, he withstood organized and violent pressure to forget".

One Day in the Life of Ivan Denisovich, for instance, is not a work of analytical history but a dawn-to-dusk window into the microscopic violations inflicted upon the person within the inhumane and hubristic Soviet prison system, captured as "one day in a drop of water" as Solzhenitsyn describes it.

Western commentators became dismissive of Solzhenitsyn's notions of memory mistaking it for a sombre and mythic nostalgia for Mother Russia. They resented his warnings of the 'forgetting of God' he saw in the West. On the 9th July 1975, Solzhenitsyn gave a speech in New York to the American Federation of Labor and Congress of Industrial Organizations and published in *Warning to the West* in which he said:

> *A handful of people determine what is good and what is bad.*
> *But I must say that in this respect Communism has been most*
> *successful. It has infected the whole world with the belief in the*
> *relativity of good and evil. Today, many people apart from the*
> *Communists are carried away by this idea.*

Russian Orthodox author and theologian Father Alexander Schmemann (1921-1983) in *Reflections on The Gulag Archipelago* observes of Solzhenitsyn's writing that it is not merely a political critique of one brutal system but, "…[a] denunciation of *all reductionism*, in revealing it as the real source of the evil which, in our contemporary world, has found its most frightening expression in the Archipelago of prisons and camps".

Solzhenitsyn in his writing places a lens over the destruction of the transcendent nature of human life evident in the grinding wheels of an ideology which is built on resentment, envy and hatred for certain groups and classes or types of life.

In his fierce acceptance speech for the Templeton prize in 1983, Solzhenitsyn locates symptoms in the butt-end of secular Western civilisation resting on the unstable culture that has rejected either a metaphysical conviction or Christian faith. He argues:

> *Such incitements to hatred are coming to characterize today's free*
> *world. Indeed, the broader the personal freedoms are, the higher*

the level of prosperity or even abundance, the more vehement,
paradoxically, is this blind hatred.

In this Templeton speech he refers to voluntary defeat in the West, a loss of a commonwealth of ethical and philosophical agreement replaced by consumption, fashion, hopelessness and a rising self-hatred, Solzhenitsyn writes, "This unquenchable hatred then spreads to all that is alive, to life itself, to the world with its colours, sounds and shapes, to the human body".

Here Solzhenitsyn's writing echoes a key theme in the teaching of Pope John Paul II, published in *Evangelium Vitae*, identifying a culture of death which attacks both human life and the human body emerging as socialised evil in both the regimes of the Soviet and in some sections of the West, "This culture is actively fostered by powerful cultural, economic and political currents which encourage an idea of society excessively concerned with efficiency".

How resonant are these warnings for the West of the 21st century.

Instead of the decaying concrete jungle of Marxist cityscapes and its prison systems we have global industries and ideologies built in stainless steel and plastic, largely adhered to by the cultural elite, but driven by socio-determinism, reductive behaviourism, transhumanism or the post-humanism of extreme ecological anxiety. Each of these abstract ideologies sprays out a wide spectrum of images and promises but they all share a cynical denial of real time virtue, transcendent thought and the importance of traditional religion.

Solzhenitsyn's Templeton speech was not simply the agitation of an older man, disillusioned by his exile from Russia. It was built on the attention he had given to the deliberate erasure of human personality, dignity and identity which took place in the Gulag system. Unlike the worship of technological tools of genocide used by Nazism or the forces in Orwell's dystopia novel *1984*, the Soviet system deployed relatively low-tech annihilation of humanity.

Despite the brutal processes of de-facing the prisoners which he experiences there, Solzhenitsyn not only survives almost miraculously, but more miraculously finds hope and faith.

Torture, punishment, over-crowding, sleep deprivation, overdoses of noise and light, strip-searches, starvation, and the leaden repetition of ideological slogans were all used to effectively fracture the personhood of the inmates and yet in the *Gulag* Solzhenitsyn remembers the importance of the soul, the reality of the divinely created Sun and the beauty of the battered human faces around him. It is in the most dire of places that he finds the gift of life. He writes, "I would come to understand many things here, Heaven! I would correct my mistakes yet, O Heaven, not for them but for you, Heaven".

In a fascinating article about the power of memory in darkest trenches and pits of suffering, the Orthodox scholar and writer, Stavros Piperis in *Memory and Commemoration in The Lord of the Rings: An Orthodox Christian Perspective* observes the power of memory in the writing of J.R.R. Tolkien's epic mythology of the *Lord of the Rings* and in Russian Christian writing:

> It rouses characters to hope in the face of staggering odds, hardening them against fear and doubt. Beyond this strengthening effect, Orthodox Christian writers also recognize memory's role in enriching and beautifying a man's life, even uniting him with God. Memory in The Lord of the Rings bears striking similarities to this idea as well.

It seems that the most insistent "canaries" are those who have walked by God's grace through the abyss of evil.

Solzhenitsyn too sees and demonstrates in his own work how artists and creative minds might offer a path through the deadening effects of totalitarianism and forgetfulness. In an interview on the BBC's *Panorama* program on March 1, 1976, Solzhenitsyn declares:

> To fight against untruth and falsehood, to fight against myths, or to fight against an ideology which is hostile to mankind, to fight for our memory, for our memory of what things were like – that is the task of the artist. A people which no longer remembers has lost its history and its soul.

The second figure exemplifying what is needed if Western culture is to survive and prosper is the English philosopher, Gertrude Elizabeth Margaret Anscombe (1918-2001). Anscombe was fiercely intelligent, and she is often held to be one of most important English-speaking philosophers of the 20th century.

Elizabeth Anscombe is one of the remarkable Oxford quartets comprising four distinctly different English women philosophers: Anscombe, Philippa Foot, Iris Murdoch and Mary Midgely. At the close of World War II this quartet breathed new urgency and humanity into the dry and abstract moral philosophy of English academe.

Elizabeth Anscombe was well known for being an eccentric unity of opposites, at least as society might judge her and about which, in any case she did not care.

She had a rigorous philosophical attention, she was a loving but absent-minded mother of seven children, a faithful Catholic who sometimes employed punchy vulgarities in the presence of Cardinals. Anscombe was a devoted protégé, translator and friend to the Austrian Ludwig Wittgenstein but one who combined his originality with a faithful engagement with the contributions of Aristotle and St Thomas Aquinas.

Anscombe's academic engagement was tough minded but original. She was an early and important opponent of the reductionism and dehumanisation of secular ethics. She thought in attentive and often demanding ways. Anscombe was intensely interested in human action and responsibility, in human dignity, in language in everyday settings and the morality and expedience of violence and killing. She publicly protested against President Truman's Oxford honours due to his role in the dropping of the atomic bomb on non-combatants in Japan at the end of World War II.

Anscombe was a major influence on Western culture as a result of her radio broadcasts and public talks and by inspiring several generations of philosophers and students to revive the significance of including virtues in any philosophical debate. She also inspired her fellow Christians by fearlessly applying her philosophy to the treatment of the unborn, the elderly and those concerned about the dangers of technology and human procreation.

Anscombe's short but vital critique of both the practical reasoning of the culture of modernity and that of the English academy of her time is captured in her treatise *Intention* published in 1957. Central to her thesis is the term she is believed to have coined, "consequentialism," when rejecting the widespread materialism of justifying certain actions by way of ends, involving the mere calculation of outcomes or consequences.

She was a pioneer in no less than Pope John Paul II's mission to re-infuse Catholic moral theology with the rigour of realistic philosophy and the inspiration of Biblical and particularly New Testament (and therefore Christological) revelation.

In his crucial encyclical *Veritatis Splendour*, John Paul II situates human intention within the wider creaturely social and cultural context, traversing concerns expressed by Elizabeth Anscombe in her earlier work on human action, His Holiness writes:

> *The primary and decisive element for moral judgment is the object of the human act, which establishes whether it is capable of being ordered to the good and to the ultimate end, which is God. This capability is grasped by reason in the very being of man, considered in his integral truth, and therefore in his natural inclinations, his motivations and his finalities, which always have a spiritual dimension as well.*

Anscombe was probably read by the Polish Pontiff before he became Pope and his concerns about ends and motivations reflect hers. One scholar of John Paul II's life notes, "One cannot imagine Karol Wojtyla writing *The Acting Person* without reading her thesis Intention – the first thing John Paul II said when anyone mentioned Oxford was, "Do you know Professor Anscombe?".

In an introductory chapter to her essays her philosopher daughter Mary Geach writes in *Human Life, Ethics and Action* that her undaunted mother considered that "philosophy is thinking about the most difficult and ultimate questions". Anscombe often framed these "ultimate" questions after encountering people in everyday non-academic settings.

Mary Geach also acknowledged that despite the apparently folksy setting of her mother's musings, Anscombe's style of philosophical argument "was dense and unrepetitive" and resembled the Italian confection panforte in that it was "chewy and tough".

Anscombe was an especially tough customer when it came to defending the dignity, purpose and value of human life. She opposed the mechanistic and materialistic accounts of human action, especially Marxism and its derivatives (now known as Woke ideology) which justified or demanded praxis based on cycles of struggle and revolution without a higher ontology of the human person.

In *The Dignity of the Human Being* Anscombe insists that, "There is just one impregnable equality of all human beings. It lies in the value and dignity of being a human being".

It is not utilitarian equations of consequences and outcomes that provide a foundation for morality but the nature of the person and his or her final fulfilment. In *Human Action* Anscombe argues:

> (M)an is spirit. He moves in the categories of innocence and answerability and desert – one of the many signs of a leap to another kind of existence from the life of the other animals.

Spirit for Anscombe is not simply an immaterial and disembodied concept but the acting and animating element which human beings share in a purposeful creaturely cosmos. This she explains in an almost whimsical essay titled *Has Mankind One Soul – An Angel Distributed Through Many Bodies*:

> There is a primary principle of the life of any kind of material living thing. I mean: a primary principle of dandelion life in a dandelion, of lion life in a lion. This primary principle I call its soul. There are also non-primary principles such as the brain of an animal or the structure of a cell.

She argues that this dignity is inherent but often only perceived by those who are virtuous or at least have the capacity and desire for virtue. In a sense this receptive virtue implies a healthy personal memory that heeds the collective memory of insights around her and particularly is open to Divine logos and end.

In this brief overview readers have been introduced to two important and enduring prophets to the memory of God's work in our world. Both as converts bring a fresh yet deeply spiritual and concrete vision to their contributions examining existential question about the meaning of life, what constitutes good and evil and how best to find fulfilment.

Such active Christians embody and witness an internalised and embodied faith which can move the mountains of absolutist, secular ideology. They give hope to the pessimistic observations of the Italian philosopher Augusto del Noce who describes the post-modern secular agenda as being an anti-theism and a "negative" faith in "sociologism".

Philosopher Michael Hanby in 'Del Noce's Moment' describes this corrosive anti-metaphysic as an invisible corrosive when he writes, "Sociologism makes anonymous atheists of us all" – even of complacent Christians their leaders and institutions.

The prophets we have thumbnailed here who live their pursuit of goodness, beauty and truth with such authenticity, disturb the waters of our cultural memory and reveal again the green edge of reasonable and charitable faith. Such prophets also bear witness to the enduring importance of Judaeo-Christianity as one of the foundation stones of Western culture.

Anna Krohn is the Executive Director of the Thomas More Centre, an Australian movement founded to form people in the principles of the common good and personal virtue and by enabling them to build supportive and intentional communities to that end.

Anna is a graduate student in theology and a student of fine art and has worked as a researcher, writer and educator in the areas of pastoral theology, healthcare ethics and in practical and professional ethics. She has worked as a columnist and on-line writer on different platforms. She has worked as a lecturer, tutor and advisor to the Australian Catholic University, The John Paul II Institute for Marriage and Family

(Melbourne), The Southern Cross Bioethics Institute in South Australia and the University of Notre Dame Australia.

Anna is also the founding convenor of the Anima Women's Network which aims to provide support and encouragement to Christian women across different age groups. In 2022 she had the honour to receive the Medal of the Order of Australia for her contributions to the Catholic Church.

Chapter Five

WESTERN CULTURE UNDER ATTACK: THE ENEMY WITHIN

Notwithstanding the unique benefits and strengths detailed in the previous chapters Western culture, and Western civilisation in general, are facing an existential threat both externally and internally. On one hand despotic, totalitarian regimes including Russia, China, Iran and North Korea threaten the West militarily. Russia's invasion of Ukraine, China threatening to invade Taiwan, Iran undertaking a proxy war against Israel and North Korea threatening South Korea and Japan are evidence freedom and liberty can no longer be assumed as sacrosanct.

The increasing use of global treaties and international agreements mandated by bodies like the World Health Organisation, the United Nations and UNESCO as well as the growth of digital monoliths including X, Meta Platforms and Google also represent a clear and present danger. What is known as the global reset also represents an ever-present danger to personal liberty and national sovereignty.

At the same time the West is being threatened externally Australia, the United Kingdom, America, New Zealand and Europe are attacked and undermined by the enemy within. Since the end of the second world war neo-Marxist inspired activists have embarked on a campaign to overthrow what they condemn as a culture guilty of racism, sexism, homophobia, transphobia, classism, Eurocentrism and white supremacy.

Instead of acknowledging the West, for all its sins and flaws, must be celebrated and defended the default position, as detailed by Roger Scruton in *Culture Counts*, is one of repudiation and condemnation. Statues of famous historical figures including Winston Churchill and Captain James Cook are graffitied and destroyed, national holidays like

Australia Day attacked and any who fail to conform to Woke ideology vilified and silenced.

As a result of post-colonial theory students are taught European explorers including Ferdinand Magellan, Christopher Columbus and Captain Cook are harbingers of oppression and exploitation instead of courageous and gifted explorers.

Students are also taught before European explorers and settlers arrived indigenous people lived a utopian life in a supposed garden of Edan free of violence and exploitation. Drawing on Rousseau's concept of the noble savage Western civilisation, on the other hand, is condemned as corrupting and exploitive.

As vividly portrayed in William Buckley's biography detailing the escaped convict's years living with Aboriginal tribes around Victoria's Port Phillip Bay, ignored is tribal life before European settlement was often characterised by violence towards women, warfare and infanticide.

Such is the irrational and one-sided nature of post-colonial theory that in the United Kingdom university students are taught there is little, if any, value in Enlightenment science as it is guilty of imperialism and colonial exploitation.

Academics at the University of Sheffield in a document titled *Decolonising the curriculum: a guide for biosciences* argue "UK science is inherently white, since the discipline developed from the European scientific enlightenment… science was both a fundamental contributor to European imperialism and a major beneficiary of its injustices".

In schools and universities young people are presented with what the Australian historian Geoffrey Blainey calls a black armband view, one that presents a bleak and depressing view of the West's institutions and history. Activists argue those academics failing to conform to their neo-Marxist ideology are guilty of Eurocentrism and white supremacy.

Instead of acknowledging it was the British government ending slavery the curriculum focuses on the European slave trade and European imperialism. Ignored are the African chieftains who terrorised and enslaved nearby tribes and the Islamic caliphate centred on the Mediterranean involved in territorial conquest and slavery.

Also rarely admitted, based on the concept of dhimmi, is the fact non-Muslims faced confiscation of property, were forced to deny their religion and were either imprisoned or killed. It should not surprise, though rarely reported, thousands of Christians in Egypt and the Middle East have been and continue to be killed.

While there is no doubt the age of imperialism, where Britain, Portugal, Spain, Holland, France and Germany competed to extend their colonial possessions leading to disease, suffering, loss and dislocation it is also true British common law and its Judaeo-Christian underpinnings exerted a positive influence.

Arriving with the First Fleet in Botany Bay in 1788 were the *King James Bible* and Blackstone's *Commentaries on the Laws of England*. Both laid the foundation for an emerging colony where the rights, liberties and freedoms we now take for granted were seeded. America's 'Declaration of Independence' is a child of Judaeo-Christianity and Enlightenment thinking.

It's no accident America's foundation document contains the phrase, "We hold these truths to be self-evident, that all men are created equal, that they are endowed by their Creator with certain unalienable Rights, that among these are Life, Liberty and the pursuit of Happiness".

The preamble to the Australian Constitution also acknowledges the central importance of Judaeo-Christianity when it states those colonies joining to form the Commonwealth of Australia do so "humbly relying on the blessing of Almighty God".

As damaging as cultural-Marxist inspired post-colonial theory is the emergence of cultural relativism and multiculturalism. Based on embracing diversity and difference the argument is new arrivals, instead of assimilating, must be given the right to live by their beliefs, religion and values.

Whether the United Kingdom, Ireland, America, Europe or Australia millions of migrants, legal and illegal, have arrived and continue to arrive establishing ghettos, importing foreign prejudices and religious feuds and, in some instances, acting as terrorists.

Instead of nation building and patriotism, essential if Western nations are to survive in an increasing hostile global environment, any who question or doubt the value of multiculturalism are condemned as racist and xenophobic.

In addition to critiquing and repudiating Western culture, Woke ideology promotes an absolutist secular vision. A vision where any sense of the spiritual and transcendent is denied and where religion, especially Judaeo-Christianity, is banished from the public square and reduced to an historical footnote.

In Australia's national curriculum from foundation to year 10 while there are literally 100s of references to indigenous culture, history and spirituality, Judaeo-Christianity is rarely, if ever, mentioned. Students leave school without any knowledge of how religion underpins and nourishes our political and legal systems and way of life.

Such is the Woke infection, anyone who publicly defends Christian beliefs is soon ostracised and cancelled, critics argue there is no place for religion when deciding government policy and religious schools, hospitals and aged care facilities must conform to a secular mandate.

In order to understand the origins of cultural-Marxism and its off springs political correctness and Woke ideology it is necessary to return to the Frankfurt School established in Germany during the late 1920s. The Marxist academics involved realised the communist revolution, while successful in Russia, was never going to happen in the West.

Notwithstanding economic downturns and depressions citizens in the West enjoyed a relatively prosperous life where they could earn a good wage, own private property and establish a business and make a profit. In Australia, the advent of the 8-hour day and a commitment to a fair and reasonable wage as a result of the Harvester Judgement also weakened revolutionary zeal.

As the workers were never going to take to the streets and storm the barricades the academics argued the most effective way to overthrow capitalism and the bourgeoisie was to take control of society's institutions including schools and universities, the church, the family, the media, political parties and intermediary organisations.

What the German radical Rudi Dutschke termed the left's long march through the institutions especially targeted universities based on the belief capitalist societies reproduce themselves by indoctrinating each generation with the belief meritocracy and competition are beneficial and worthwhile.

Central to the Frankfurt School's long march is critical theory. Instead of knowledge being good in itself and directed at beauty, wisdom and truth, critical theory argues the only worthwhile learning is that which is liberating and emancipatory in nature.

Knowledge and learning are critiqued in terms of power relationships involving sexuality, gender, ethnicity, race and class. The purpose of education is to critique capitalist, Western societies and to reveal how citizens, even though they might think otherwise, are deluded and oppressed.

Cultural-left activists argue academic success is based on socioeconomic status instead of ability, motivation and the willingness to work hard. Working class students who believe with effort and application they can achieve academic success ignore the fact only wealthy and privileged students do well.

Instead of a grand narrative view of history, beginning with ancient civilisations including Mesopotamia, Egypt, Greece and Rome and based on the belief civilisation has improved, students are taught to condemn Western civilisation as inherently oppressive and destructive.

Whereas literature once centred on those well-crafted and enduring works saying something profound and enduring about human nature and the world in which they live students are told to analyse how texts either ignore or marginalise the oppressed.

Two Marxist academics associated with the Frankfurt School who have had, and continue to have, a profound impact on Western culture are Herbert Marcuse and Wilhelm Reich. Marcuse in 'Repressive Tolerance' argues Western societies are so corrupt and oppressive those seeking radical change have every right to be intolerant.

Marcuse writes "what is proclaimed and practiced as tolerance today, is in many of its most effective manifestations serving the cause of oppression". As a result, those fighting to reshape society are permitted any means, no matter how offensive, violent or illegal, in order to achieve the desired outcome.

As previously argued by Vladimir Lenin, "Morality is whatever brings about the success of the proletarian revolution". In a world driven by communist ideology virtues like love, honesty, truth and commitment to human flourishing and the common good are ignored and seen as dispensable.

Equally concerning is the argument rationality and reason are disposable as such concepts are Eurocentric, binary and guilty of reinforcing capitalist hegemony. Critical thinking and objectivity give way to emotion and the belief "I feel, therefore I'm right".

Such is the power of Marcuse's call for intolerance any who dare to question or fail to conform to Woke ideology are attacked, vilified, no-platformed and cancelled. As argued by Camille Paglia in *Free Women Free Men*, "We are plunged once again into an ethical chaos where intolerance masquerades as tolerance and where individual liberty is crushed by the tyranny of the group".

As noted by the Italian cultural critic and philosopher Augusto Del Noce in *The Crisis of Modernity*, Wilhelm Reich's book the *Sexual Revolution* represents another significant attack on Western culture and how people perceive themselves and interact with others.

Unlike classical Marxism focusing on the modes and means of production, Reich argues the most effective way to overthrow capitalism is to undertake a sexual revolution. Instead of the workers freeing their economic chains, Reich believes sexual repression is the main cause of injustice and lack of freedom.

He writes that "an individual who is sexually happy does not need an inhibiting 'morality' or the supernatural 'religious experience'. Basically, life is as simple as that. It becomes complicated only by the human structure which is characterized by the fear of life".

Marcuse is especially critical of what he terms the "patriarchal-authoritarian family" and writes "...in the process of the social revolution the old form of the family will inevitably disintegrate". For this to occur society must allow adolescent sexual freedom and religion must stop imposing "sexual anxiety and sexual guilt feelings".

Frank Knopfelmacher in *Selected Writings* describes Marcuse's theory as follows:

> *Church, school, official morality – but particularly the fetters*
> *of Judeo-Christian monogamous family – are holding human*
> *sexuality in chains, serving thereby as neurosis-inducing agencies*
> *perpetuating the psychological hegemony of the ruling class*
> *over the masses. Thus, the socialist revolution must be preceded*
> *by sexual emancipation, because the former is psychologically*
> *impossible with the later...*

While the English version of *The Sexual Revolution* was published in 1951 his work was rediscovered during the cultural revolution of the late 1960s and early 1970s. This was a time when slogans like "make love, not war" and "turn on, tune in and drop out" were taken literally and young people across the West championed a licentious, alternative lifestyle in opposition to what was condemned as an oppressive and authoritarian system.

In 1965 Dr John Money established a gender clinic at John Hopkins University heralding the belief gender is a social construct. As a result, puberty blockers and life changing surgery are allowed for adolescents suffering gender dysphoria ignoring the reality gender and sexuality are biologically determined and God given.

Similar to Wilhelm Reich, the champion of Australia's Safe Schools gender fluidity program, Roz Ward, justifies teaching boys can be girls and girls can be boys by drawing on Marxist ideology. Ward argues, "Marxism offers both the hope and the strategy needed to create a world where human sexuality, gender and how we relate to our bodies can blossom in extraordinary, new and amazing ways that we can only try to imagine today".

The cultural revolution of the late1960s and early 1970s, in addition to experiencing a sexual revolution, was also a time when postmodernism, deconstructionism and gender, post-colonial and transgender theories began to infect schools and universities.

This rainbow alliance of critical theories, while different in many ways, are all alike in that they represent a fundamental attack on Western culture and Western civilisation. Concepts like objectivity and truth are condemned as binary and oppressive and the belief knowledge and wisdom are beneficial likewise denounced.

Relativism and subjectivity prevail, as does the belief all discourse is based on power relationships. As noted by Roger Scruton, "Truth, Foucault tells us, is not an absolute, which can be understood and assessed, in some trans-historical way… Truth is the child of 'discourse', and as discourse changes, so does the truth contained in it".

Greek tragedies, Shakespeare's plays, T.S. Eliot's poetry and the writings of Jane Austen and Patrick White, for example, are critiqued and analysed in terms of power relationships involving class, gender, sexuality, ethnicity and race. The Bible, instead of revealing the word of God, is merely another text that must be deconstructed in terms of critical theory.

As a result of deconstructionism how one interprets texts has also been radically altered. Schools and universities teach there is no authorial intent as the author is dead and works like Shakespeare's *Romeo and Juliet* and Joseph Conrad's *Heart of Darkness* are open to a multitude of meanings as how one interprets a text is fluid and dynamic. (Except, of course, when Woke ideology is invoked where there is only one correct interpretation based on neo-Marxist inspired critical theory.)

Debasing language and using it to enforce groupthink and mind control is another destructive result of critical theory and Woke ideology. The author of *1984*, George Orwell, argues if thought can control language, then language can control thought. Orwell also writes manipulating and using language is a strategy commonly used by dictators to impose conformity.

In the world of Big Brother and the Ministry of Truth Orwell gives the example of the slogan "War is peace, freedom is slavery and ignorance is strength". Coupled with hate sessions, fear of the Thought Police and the threat of imprisonment and torture, citizens are incapable of independent thought and the ability to question authority and act independently.

Language control to enforce group think is especially present with gender and sexuality theory. Breast feeding is replaced by chest feeding, father by non-gestational parent and cervix with front hole. Descriptions like women and men and girls and boys are also criticised as imposing a binary, heteronormative view of sexuality.

Language is also used to shut down debate and to silence any who question or disagree with the prevailing Woke orthodoxy. Question multiculturalism and you are condemned as racist and xenophobic, argue women can be attractive and you are sexist and misogynist. Suggesting Western culture is worth acknowledging and defending and you are attacked as a white supremacist.

Corporations, universities and government departments have all drunk the Kool-Aid when it comes to enforcing language control and group think. Diversity and inclusiveness guides are common where pronouns like he/she and descriptions like husband/wife and mother/father are cancelled.

Such is the debilitating and destructive nature of language control Roger Scruton in *Conservatism* notes how prescient Orwell was and writes:

> *The humourless and relentless policing of language, so as to prevent heretical thoughts from arising, the violence done to traditional categories and natural ways of describing things, the obliteration of memory and assiduous policing of the past – all of these things, so disturbingly described in Nineteen Eighty-Four, are now routinely to be observed on university campuses on both sides of the Atlantic.*

Since the time of the French Revolution, it has been generally accepted to refer to the left and the right when distinguishing between political parties and their beliefs. The concept is traced to those defending the monarch who sat to the right-hand side of the assembly's president and those who sat on the left-hand side committed to radical change.

Since the Russian Revolution the terms left and right have become common place when describing political parties. In Australia, the Liberal/National parties are seen as centre-right, while the Australian Labor Party and the Greens Party are described as centre-left. In America, the distinction is between the left-leaning Democrats and the right-leaning Republicans.

While much of the political and social debate is couched in terms of left and right, as argued by Del Noce, such descriptions fail to address what has become a new form of totalitarianism threatening Western culture and civilisation.

The distinction between socialism and communism and between cultural-Marxism and conservatism, while still relevant, fails to address what Del Noce in an essay titled 'Toward a New Totalitarianism' published in *The Crisis of Modernity* describes as the dangers represented by scientism and the technological society.

While acknowledging the benefits of science Del Noce warns about the destructive impact of scientism. This he describes as a:

> ... *totalitarianism conception of science, in which science is regarded as the only true form of knowledge. According to this view, every other type of knowledge – metaphysical or religious – expresses only 'subjective reactions', which we are able, or will be able, to explain by extending science to the human sphere through psychological and sociological research.*

Scientism is based on the belief the only things that are true are those that can be quantified and measured. The world is a temporal one where with enough ingenuity, skill and knowledge it is possible to shape what it means to be human and to control the physical world.

Denying the God given and biological nature of gender and sexuality, believing humans can control climate change, gain-of-function research associated with the Covid-19 pandemic as well as abortion on demand, legalising state sanctioned suicide and opening a Pandora's box represented by AI highlight the dangers of scientism.

Associated with scientism is the technological society; a society that condemns the past as obsolete and irrelevant, denies any sense of the spiritual and transcendent and defines human nature and the world in which we live in terms of its material value and utility.

In education, priority is given to vague and generalised work-related skills and competencies summed up by the expression 21st century, life-long learning. What Matthew Arnold terms "the best that has been thought and said" is criticised as obsolete and backward looking.

Virtues such as wisdom, beauty and truth give way to a soulless and barren world where individuals are subsumed by the collective and where liberty and freedom are replaced by mind control and group think.

As argued by Oxford's Baroness Susan Greenfield and, more recently, Jonathan Haidt in *The Anxious Generation*, the technological society's dependence on computers, screens and mobile phones has had a destructive effect on generations of young people addicted to the virtual world.

Research proves computer screens and the digital world, as well as denying the ability to meet and socialise face to face, adversely impact on children's cognitive development. Too many students enter school incapable of concentrating on the printed word and unable to work diligently for long periods of time.

As parents are beginning to find out, mobile phones represent a Faustian bargain where vulnerable children and teenagers are open to a dark and dehumanising world involving sexting, cyber bullying, sextortion and mental and emotional abuse.

Australia's response to the Covid-19 pandemic illustrates the destructive nature of scientism and the dangers inherent in a technological society. In addition to the Australian government shutting the nation's borders, thus denying the right citizens have to return home, politicians and health officials created a climate of fear and dread calculated to frighten people into obedience.

Interstate travel was stopped, curfews imposed and travel outside the home made illegal. As a result, people were denied the right to visit sick and dying family and relatives, children lost weeks and months of schooling and small businesses were bankrupted and people's careers destroyed.

In Victoria, the then premier Daniel Andrews (aka dictator Dan) acted as a one-man government trouncing Westminster parliamentary conventions and cancelling long defended liberties and freedoms. Police violence became widespread with peaceful protestors pepper sprayed and at least on one occasion shot at with rubber bullets.

Andrews, much like Big Brother in Orwell's *1984*, enforced obedience by projecting concern and sympathy as the state's guardian and protector while employing doublethink and fear to ensure compliance. The slogan "staying apart, keeps us together" became the government's mantra and the premier constantly portrayed the pandemic as a deadly beast.

Worst of all, notwithstanding the lack of medical evidence and proper trials, experimental vaccines pushed by global pharmaceutical companies became compulsory in order for teachers, hospital workers, police and emergency personnel to keep their jobs.

No surprisingly, in a speech titled *A State Of Fear* given to the Melbourne-based Robert Menzies Institute the United Kingdom's Lord Jonathan Sumption argues events in Australia, and other Western nations, demonstrate how fragile democracies are and how liberties and freedoms can so easily be lost.

By injecting fear and mass psychosis to control citizens Sumption warns "…the use of political power as an instrument of mass coercion fuelled by public fear is corrosive". Indeed, such is the threat Sumption concludes his talk by suggesting the West is "entering a Hobbesian world, the enormity of which has not yet downed on our people".

In the years since the spread of the Covid-19 virus especially disconcerting is that fears expressed at the time about government overreach and the safety and efficacy of mRNA vaccines have been justified. Medical and education experts now admit closing schools for extended periods has caused more harm to students than good.

American's health official Dr Anthony Fauci most responsible for justifying draconian measures now admits wearing masks was not very effective in preventing infection and AstraZeneca, after withdrawing its vaccine from global distribution, now admits it can cause adverse medial reactions including fatal blood clots.

Whether as a result of what doctors are calling long Covid, or as some argue the harmful after effects of Covid-19 vaccines, there has been a significant increase in people suffering serious medical conditions including neurological disorders, fatigue, myocarditis and pericarditis.

Such is the destructive nature of neo-Marxist inspired Woke ideology, incorporating postmodernism, deconstructionism and radical feminist, gender and post-colonial theories, that even those associated with the centre-left are warning about its extreme, intolerant and unacceptable nature.

President Obama in a speech to college students warns about holding views that polarise issues as either right or wrong and automatically condemn opponents as the enemy. In an open letter to *Harper's Magazine* titled *A Letter on Justice and Open Debate* over 100 noted authors and writers argue public discourse is characterised by "… an intolerance of opposing views, a vogue for public shaming and ostracism, and the tendency to dissolve complex policy issues in a blinding moral certainty".

While such criticism is directed at the "radical right" the letter also warns those on the left that "The democratic inclusion we want can be achieved only if we speak out against the intolerant climate that has set in on all sides". An open and free society only exists if tolerance, rationality and reason prevail.

As history tells us, one of the unique strengths and benefits of Western culture is the belief it is possible to more closely approximate the truth of things and to have reasoned debate. The only alternatives are violence, epistemological suicide or silence.

Dr Kevin Donnelly, since first warning about the dangers of politically correct language control and group think in the mid-1990s, has established himself, in the words of Sky News' Peta Credlin, as "one of Australia's foremost culture war warriors". He is a vocal defender of Western civilisation and Judeo-Christianity against the destructive and nihilistic impact of neo-Marxist inspired Woke ideology. He writes regularly for the print and digital media, including: The Australian, The Daily Telegraph, The Catholic Weekly, Quadrant, the Australian Spectator and the London based Conservative Woman.

Kevin also appears regularly on Sky News and books published include: The Dictionary Of Woke, Cancel Culture and the Left's Long March, Christianity Matters In These Troubled Times, How Political Correctness Is Destroying Australia. How Political Correctness Is Destroying Education. Educating Your Child: It's Not Rocket Science and The Culture Of Freedom. Kevin's website is kevindonnelly.com.au In 2014 Kevin co-chaired a review of the Australian National Curriculum and in 2016 he received an Order of Australia for services to education.

Chapter Six

THE SELF-HATING AGE: HOW OIKOPHOBIA IS DECAYING THE WEST

Societal critique is a central pillar of the Western inheritance. Plato's *Republic* and Aristotle's *Politics* assess the most fundamental aspects of civilisation and seek to describe the ideal society. Moreover, the Old Testament contains a commentary on the historical development of the Israelites, and its prophets admonish the rich for neglecting the poor. Honest, often harsh, self-criticism is embedded in the Western tradition. Indeed, it is a core means by which our civilisation has flourished over the centuries, from the Medieval era, through the Enlightenment, and into Modernity.

Yet, over the preceding decades, this tradition of thoughtful, constructive critique has been transmogrified into a poisonous campaign against the heart of Western culture. The very organisation of our societies – from the class structure and the family to the economic model – has been under sustained assault. The attack manifests in various modes of pseudo-intellectual 'deconstruction', which seek to present the Western status quo, and the history from which it was forged, as innately wicked and repressive.

Although this is now familiar to us in the form of the prevailing Woke ideology, the true origins of this attack can be traced to the early part of the twentieth century (and, indeed, earlier); but the campaign of grievance and civilisational self-hatred has in recent decades usurped our intellectual traditions to become the dominant mode of Western thought.

In his 2004 book *England and the Need for Nations*, the British philosopher Roger Scruton termed the rising liberal ideology of self-contempt as "oikophobia". The Ancient Greek word for home is *oikos*; and thus oikophobia, Scruton wrote, is "(stretching the Greek a little) the repudiation of inheritance and home." It manifests as a consolidated, wide-spanning offensive against the historical, theological, literary, legal and social inheritance that formed the modern West.

The intellectual engine driving oikophobia is a set of critical theories that seek to deconstruct (simply: attack) our history, our justice system, our political traditions, and so forth. The essential pillars of our civilisation are smeared by the Left's creedal oppressor-victim narrative – a simplistic, catch-all lens through which some powerful group is claimed to have exploited and repressed some weaker group. By the lights of this Manichean and warped rubric, the very essence of Western society is castigated as irredeemably wicked.

As Scruton observed:

> *Oikophobia is a stage through which the adolescent mind normally passes. But it is a stage in which some people – the intellectuals especially – tend to become arrested. As George Orwell pointed out, intellectuals on the Left are especially prone to it, and this has often made them willing agents of foreign powers.*

Hence, the tedious political activism that was formerly confined to the university campus has now been propagated across Western institutions and corporations. Indeed, the touted 'grown-ups' in the West are now largely liberal oikophobes, educated at elite universities that serve, as the conservative historian Niall Ferguson has argued, to transmit civilisational self-contempt in place of the classical Western inheritance.

Scruton observed that the Left's oikophobic movement was cultivated in Western universities over decades. It was propelled especially by the Frankfurt School, a leftwing academic circle that originated in the Weimar Republic of the interwar period. Critically, its founding thinkers moved to American universities during the 1930s, within which they exerted a profound and lasting influence.

Writers such as Theodor Adorno, Jürgen Habermas and Herbert Marcuse decried the institutions, and the very structure, of Western culture as inherently oppressive. Although now obscure, these thinkers guided the thought of important – and vastly overrated – leftwing giants of the late twentieth century such as Michel Foucault and Jacques Derrida, who in turn formed the modern leftwing intellectual paradigm. The Frankfurt School thus began a surreptitious and longstanding war against the foundations of Western culture from inside its finest academic institutions.

In his excellent book *Fools, Frauds and Firebrands: Thinkers of the New Left*, Scruton dismantles the intellectual "nonsense machine" created by the modern Left. He observes that, according to the leftwing rubric, "The condition of society is essentially one of domination, in which people are bound to each other by their attachments and distinguished by rivalries and competition". Formerly, it was social class and economic relations that defined the Left's interpretation of the Western power-struggle. But following the end of the Cold War and the blatant collapse of the socialist economic model, the Left forged new cultural fault-lines out of race, sex and sexuality. This politics of personal identity eventually evolved into the Woke dialectic which now dominates our universities with its crude caricatures and biases. Indeed, it has been through the Left's longstanding capture of these prominent institutions that the oikophobic ideology has been imparted to the Western elite – and hence to society writ large.

Importantly, this is not the first time that the intelligentsia has led Western societies dangerously astray. In a recent essay titled 'The Treason of the Intellectuals', Niall Ferguson illustrates the parallels between the Left's ideological capture of the modern university and the leading role played by German academics in the Nazi movement. He writes:

> *Non-Jewish German academia did not just follow Hitler down the path to hell. It led the way… Anyone who has a naive belief in the power of higher education to instil ethical values has not studied the history of German universities in the Third Reich. A university degree, far from inoculating Germans against Nazism, made them more likely to embrace it.*

Thus, Nazism was not a movement of working-class troglodytes against the learned elite; it was in fact the bien-pensant ideology *of* the elite. Ferguson continues:

> *Later, after it was all over, the historian Friedrich Meinecke tried to explain "the German catastrophe" by arguing that excessive technical specialization had caused some educated Germans (not him, needless to say) to lose sight of the humanistic values of Goethe and Schiller. As a result, they had been unable to resist Hitler's "mass Machiavellianism".*

This same excessive specialisation has corrupted modern Western universities. As the American classicist Victor Davis Hanson observes, "special studies courses" have diluted curricula, distracting students – and their professors – from the difficult, traditional subjects of law, history, philosophy, and so forth. Hence, the academic elite is exponentially distancing itself from the Western moral and intellectual inheritance, leaving a vacuum that is being steadily filled by oikophobic grievance studies that attack the core of our civilisation.

So, what forms does the modern oikophobic assault against the West take? The campaign is waged on four principal battlefronts: First, Western history is condemned in an ahistorical, gratuitously unfair, even *smirking*, manner. European colonialism is presented as a purely racist endeavour, dismissing and denying all its moral and material complexity.

Similarly, the greatest figures of the modern West – including Winston Churchill, the American Founding Fathers, and Abraham Lincoln – are besmirched as incorrigible oppressors and racists who fail the modern, *specifically leftwing* morality-tests. It is obvious that the aim is not to revise history in the spirit of curiosity and truth, but rather to disparage and poison the heroes and events that anchor us to a nation and to a collective past. In short, it is designed to sever us from the very roots of our civilisation, thereby creating an historical *tabula rasa* onto which a new utopian society can be inscribed.

Second, the theological basis of the modern West – Christianity –

has been assailed ferociously by the secular Left. The attack gained
momentum through the twentieth century, culminating in the popular
New Atheist movement of the early 2000s. Although its leading
thinkers, all secular liberals, claimed to denigrate all religions equally,
it was in fact the Old and New Testaments, and the Catholic Church
especially, that received the brunt of its ire.

Moreover, the modern Left shows consistent bias towards Islam
and other non-Western religions, whilst agitating fervently against
Christianity and the cultural influence it has traditionally wielded.
Indeed, this theological attack is a foundational pillar of the oikophobic
campaign; for it was through our Christian heritage that the moral
and social cosmos of the West was formed. And it is therefore only
by breaking our allegiance to that cosmos that the new, 'progressive'
morality of the Left can be imposed.

Third, contempt for traditional customs and simple patriotism has
become a familiar and undisguised trait of the oikophobic Left. Indeed,
George Orwell recognised the roots of this adolescent sentiment in his
great 1941 essay, *England Your England*. He wrote:

> *In left-wing circles it is always felt that there is something slightly*
> *disgraceful in being an Englishman and that it is a duty to snigger*
> *at every English institution, from horse racing to suet puddings. It is*
> *a strange fact, but it is unquestionably true that almost any English*
> *intellectual would feel more ashamed of standing to attention*
> *during 'God Save the King' than of stealing from a poor box.*

Such absurd antipathy has only worsened; increasingly in the West,
the metropolitan, monied upper-classes are dissociating themselves
from the largely provincial, poorer working-classes. This manifests
in an enduring attack on tradition and patriotism. In Britain, for
example, the English flag and St George's Day are increasingly treated
as symbols of pseudo-fascism by smug, university-educated liberals.
In America, too, the sentiments and loyalties of ordinary people –
particularly those of the Rust Belt and the Deep South – are sneered at
by the bicoastal, metropolitan Left.

Fourth, as Orwell further noted in *England Your England*, a chief symptom of the Left's worldview is its servility to anti-Western foreign regimes. In Orwell's day, members of the Left were beguiled by Stalin's Soviet Union, denying or excusing its appalling crimes. Today, we see the Left's chronic apologism for Iran's dangerous aggressions in the Middle East. China – a repressive, imperialist, post-communist dystopia – is treated with absurd sympathy, too.

These strange allegiances are motivated by the familiar leftwing dogma which states that foreign cultures must not be criticised; but it is also part of a juvenile and spiteful compulsion on the Left to side with whatever is not Western *against* the West. Perhaps the most outrageously hateful personification of this oikophobic preference for foreign agents is the overt support for Hamas among many pampered young activists at American and European universities. Much of this shocking outburst is certainly anti-Semitic. But it is, above all, specifically anti-Western and oikophobic in its origin and intent. Israel is monstered by leftwing radicals precisely because it is a Western, democratic, free, prosperous enclave surrounded by hostile and repressive non-Western neighbours. Such radicals are indeed the pro-Stalinists of our time.

Why has oikophobia emerged in our civilisation – and why is it accelerating? Crucially, the oikophobic attack has recurred throughout Western history. In his 2022 book *Western Self-Contempt: Oikophobia in the Decline of Civilizations*, the philosopher Dr Benedict Beckeld observes that the elites of Ancient Athens and Rome became openly contemptuous of their own civilisations during the latter stages of their respective declines. In both societies, it was a phenomenon of the elites and the intellectual class. It was not shared by the people at large, who continued, broadly, to uphold the conservative, patriotic traditions by which the state and society had been served and respected.

Beckeld argues that, in a civilisation's early days, its confidence rides high; yet, once external enemies have been defeated, and as decadence, leisure, egalitarianism, and individual empowerment set in, new internal enemies and regressive political machinations are crafted. Thus, writes Beckeld, "success is, ironically, a prerequisite for a society's self-hatred."

The modern oikophobic attack on the West should thus be interpreted as both a symptom and a cause of our own steady decline. The sense of self-contempt, downturn and moral guilt was exacerbated by the great catastrophes of the last century: the world wars; financial and imperial decline; the Holocaust; the 1960s social revolutions; and the calamity in Vietnam. These all undermined Western moral and civilisational confidence, lending credence to the budding preachers of self-hatred. However, as the oikophobic intellectual attack has taken ever-bolder shape, it has itself served to profoundly accelerate and deepen our decline by fragmenting Western peoples along cultural lines and corrupting the hearts of our most valuable institutions.

The only remedy is to recover the true roots of the Western intellectual heritage. Criticism must once again, in the spirit of Plato and Aristotle, serve to advance our civilisation, not smear and dismantle it. Reconstruction begins in our universities, where the traditions of free inquiry and the rigorous pursuit of truth must be retrieved. Our other institutions will follow the academics' lead – just as they have done historically.

So, as Roger Scruton advised shortly before his death, we must simply stop listening to the Left's high priests that currently sit enthroned in the Western Academy, and recover our higher inheritance.

A. Gibson

Chapter Seven

THE TIDE IS TURNING –
A GLOBAL PERSPECTIVE

While history is often recounted through the lens of battles and great leaders, the truth is that the real engine behind the rise and fall of civilizations is culture. Whether a society embraces its values, loses itself in cynicism, or revitalises its institutions, the cultural undercurrent tells you more about where things are headed than any battlefield victory ever could. Andrew Breitbart once said, "Politics is downstream from culture," and he was spot on. If you want to see where the wind's blowing, look at a civilisation's culture, because that's where it all starts before spilling over into legislation.

Let's be clear, cultural change rarely comes from one individual. It's the work of networks, groups of like-minded people who push their worldview forward that change the status quo.

In this chapter, we're going to take a look at a small snapshot of some of the cultural movements that have sprung up around the world, the unlikely alliances that have formed in the name of truth, and the networks that have grown stronger because of them. We'll also touch on some legislative victories that suggest the tide might be turning. The battle is far from won, but there's definitely momentum building against the cultural-Marxist inspired ideology that has captured our institutions, and Australians should feel encouraged that we can replicate this work here.

But first, how did we get in this mess? And how have new technologies given us the tools we need to push back against the tide?

For centuries, the flow of information was controlled by two institutions, the local monarch, and the church. But with the printing press, information became democratised, those traditional gatekeepers lost their stranglehold on the public square, and Pandora's box was unleashed. This led to generations of power struggles and revolutions. The church split, monarchs were overthrown and in time, Europe (and the rest of the world) came to resemble the status quo of today.

Fast forward to the 20th century, and mass media companies took over as the new gatekeepers. Governments set up state broadcasters like the BBC and ABC, but control of the narrative stayed firmly in the hands of a few institutions.

Despite these large corporate and government controlled gatekeepers, localism in the media mostly meant diverse perspectives. Journalists started at the grassroots and worked their way up based on merit, and the media largely worked in common step with the people and their values. But then journalism became professionalised, universities became the new training grounds for broadcasters, and the stage was set for the long march through the institutions.

The game plan went something like this: capture the arts faculty, then the education faculty, followed by the journalism and media courses. Indoctrinate the next generation of teachers, rewrite the curriculums, and populate the media with activists and voilà, you've got a public square filled with radical, post-modern, deconstructive, and Woke ideas.

But this story doesn't have to end here, thanks to a little invention even more revolutionary than the printing press, the internet. The internet has blown the legacy gatekeepers out of the water. It's given dissident voices a platform to challenge the cultural dominance of cultural-left ideologues. YouTube, podcasts, and online programming have democratised access to information, creating a diversity of content that's never been seen before. The United States has led the charge in reaching massive audiences with this dissident content, but the United Kingdom and Europe through long form broadcasters and social commentators are hot on their heels.

So, if you're worried about where things are headed, remember this, culture is up for grabs, and it's ours to shape. The internet has levelled the playing field, and with the right approach, we can push back against the cultural tide and steer the ship in a better direction.

The cultural landscape has been turned on its head by the rise of a group of dissident voices who've done the unthinkable, they've actually dared to say what they think. But instead of being banished to the wilderness, these figures, Joe Rogan, Jordan Peterson, and the band of misfits known as the Intellectual Dark Web (IDW), have managed to carve out new spaces for dialogue and debate. And let's not forget Elon Musk, the billionaire who decided to take on the digital censors by buying Twitter and turning it into X, a fortress for free speech. So, what did they do? How did they do it? And why should anyone who's tired of walking on ideological eggshells care? Let's dive in.

First up, Joe Rogan. Now, Rogan's not exactly your typical hero. He's a comedian who likes to punch people in the face for fun and then talk about it for three hours on his podcast, *The Joe Rogan Experience.* But here's the thing , Rogan's show isn't just about laughs and UFC highlights. It's become the go-to place for long-form, unfiltered conversations. Rogan invites all sorts of people, from scientists and philosophers to those who've been cast out by the mainstream media, and he gives them the time and space to actually explain their views.

No soundbites, no interruptions, just real, deep conversations. And people love it. Why? Because in a world where the news is spoon-fed to us in 30-second clips, Rogan's podcast is a refreshing blast of fresh air. He's bypassed the usual media gatekeepers and created a platform where alternative perspectives can flourish. The result? Millions of listeners who are fed up with being told what to think now have a place where they can hear the other side.

Then we have Jordan Peterson, the Canadian professor who catapulted to fame after refusing to comply with Canada's compelled speech laws. These laws would have forced people to use specific gender pronouns, and Peterson said, 'Not on my watch'. That simple act of defiance resonated with people around the world, especially those who recognised that compelled speech leads to a slippery slope of eroded rights and freedoms. Peterson didn't just stop at saying 'no'. He offered a positive alternative through his book, *12 Rules for Life,* which is all about taking personal responsibility and finding meaning in a chaotic world.

His message has struck a chord with young men who feel lost in today's society, but it's also earned him a place as a symbol of resistance against ideological conformity. Thanks to appearances on Rogan's show and his own relentless lecture tours, Peterson has become a leading voice in the pushback against Woke culture.

Both Rogan and Peterson have become mainstream figures in a group termed 'the Intellectual Dark Web', or IDW for short. This involves a loose collection of thinkers, people like Sam Harris, Ben Shapiro, Eric Weinstein, and Heather Heying who share one thing in common, they're not afraid to challenge the orthodoxies of political correctness. These folks aren't just whining about Woke culture; they're creating spaces where real, complex conversations can happen without the fear of being cancelled.

Take Ben Shapiro's *Daily Wire*, for example. It's become one of the fastest-growing media outlets in the U.S., offering a clear alternative to the mainstream narrative. The IDW's influence has been growing, despite (or perhaps because of) the significant pushback they've faced. Many of the commentators have been deplatformed, but they've refused to be silenced.

Enter Elon Musk, the man who decided that enough was enough and bought Twitter. Now rebranded as X, Musk's takeover wasn't just a business move, it was a declaration of war against the digital censors. He reinstated banned accounts, fired the executives who enforced censorship, and made it clear that X would be a platform for free speech.

Musk also opened up Twitter's inner workings to investigative journalists Matt Taibi, Michael Shellenberger and Bari Weiss who revealed the now infamous *Twitter Files*. Taibi, Shellenberger and Weiss uncovered that Twitter's top brass were playing a bit of a puppet master game, quietly deciding which voices got amplified and which ones were silenced. They weren't just moderating for 'hate speech' or 'harmful content'; they were manipulating political discussions, nudging conversations in certain directions, and even making calls that influenced major news events such as the suppression of the now confirmed Hunter Biden laptop story. Twitter was acting as a speech referee that wasn't just enforcing their own Silicon Valley echo chamber rules, they were changing them as they went along, all while keeping us in the dark.

Musk has now turned Twitter into a frontline in the battle against ideological conformity. His actions have emboldened others who felt silenced by the digital gatekeepers, proving that it's possible to fight back and win.

Rogan, Peterson, the IDW, and Musk didn't just complain about the state of things; they built their own platforms, connected directly with their audiences, and created spaces where free thought can flourish. They've broken the monopoly that Woke ideology had over public discourse and proved that there's a massive audience out there hungry for something different.

For Australians looking for inspiration, the lesson is clear; you don't need to wait for permission to speak your mind. Whether it's starting a podcast, writing a blog, or simply engaging in more thoughtful conversations on social media, the tools to push back are already in your hands. Be bold, be thoughtful, and don't be afraid to challenge the status quo. If Rogan, Peterson, Musk, and the IDW can do it on the global stage, there's no reason we can't do it right here at home.

If we're going to stand a chance in this culture war against Woke madness, we need cross-cultural and cross-political alliances, where people from all walks of life and political stripes come together for the common cause of common sense. It's like being in a pub quiz team where you've got the brainiac, the sports nut, and the guy who knows every obscure fact about 80s music, all different, but together, unstoppable. Because, let's face it, this isn't just about left versus right anymore. It's about preserving common sense, freedom of speech, and the ability to have a conversation without someone trying to get you fired for it. After all, if we don't hang together, as the saying goes, we'll most certainly hang separately.

With echo chambers becoming increasingly siloed, one group that managed to break out of the ossified left/right divide in the UK has been the movement of the Trans Exclusionary Radical Feminists, or TERF's. And perhaps the two most high profile TERF's are Kathleen Stock and J.K. Rowling.

So, what have Kathleen Stock and J.K. Rowling done that's got everyone from left to right rallying around them? Quite simply, they've stood their ground in the face of what can only be described as an ideological steamroller. Stock, a British philosopher, dared to argue that biological sex actually matters, shocking, I know, especially in a world increasingly obsessed with identity politics and the idea that you are whatever you say you are. Meanwhile, J.K. Rowling, the creator of a wizarding empire, had the audacity to tweet that women are, well, women. For these crimes against Woke orthodoxy, they've both been dragged over the coals, but here's the kicker; they didn't back down. And in not backing down, they've done something far more significant than just defending their own views, they've become rallying points for a much larger world-wide pushback.

How did they manage this? By being, quite frankly, unflappable. Stock was hounded out of her academic job by students who thought that setting off smoke bombs near her office was a reasonable response to academic debate. Rather than grovelling for forgiveness, she doubled down, argued her case publicly, and drew support from over 200 academics who finally decided they'd had enough. Friendlies in the conservative media picked up the story, and before long, the government was introducing legislation to protect free speech on campuses. Not bad for someone who was supposed to be cancelled.

Rowling, on the other hand, faced death threats and calls for boycotts after she dared to suggest that women might have rights worth protecting. But instead of issuing a tearful apology, she wrote a detailed essay laying out her concerns with the precision of a lawyer and the passion of someone who genuinely cares about the issue. Her stance drew support from all corners, from conservative pundits to left-wing feminists who've also had it up to here with the Woke brigade. In both cases, the key was sticking to their guns, speaking clearly, and refusing to be bullied into silence.

So, why does this matter for those looking to push back against Woke culture? The lesson here is that courage is contagious. Stock and Rowling didn't just defend their views; they emboldened others to speak out too. When people see that it's possible to survive, and even thrive, after standing up to the mob, it encourages them to do the same.

For Australians looking for inspiration, the takeaway is simple; don't be afraid to speak up. The cultural tides can seem overwhelming, but as Stock and Rowling have shown, they're not unstoppable. When you stand firm and articulate your position with clarity and conviction, you can rally support even from the most unlikely quarters. The key is to be unyielding in your principles while making your case as clearly and reasonably as possible. If the Brits can do it in the face of campus mobs and Twitter storms, then we, in Australia, can do it too.

While the European Union might be better known for its endless regulations and wonky cheese laws, there's been a quiet revolution brewing on the right side of the political spectrum. Over the last few years, right-leaning parties have been making serious inroads, shaking up the status quo and giving the legacy metropolitan globalist elites a run for their money.

Across the continent, conservative movements are rising, fuelled by a growing dissatisfaction with the cultural-Marxist inspired politically correct policies that have dominated for years. But how did we get here? And why should anyone looking to push back against Woke culture care? Let's dive in.

First up, the Red Wall in Britain. Now, for those not in the know, the Red Wall refers to a string of working-class areas in the Midlands, North of England, and Wales that had been as loyal to the Labour Party as a dog is to its owner. But in 2019, something extraordinary happened – these voters switched sides, backing Boris Johnson and the Conservatives. It wasn't just about Brexit, though that certainly played a part. It was about a growing sense of cultural dislocation, a feeling that Labour had abandoned its roots in favour of progressive, elitist metropolitan values that didn't resonate with the people who actually live in these areas.

This wasn't just a political shift; it was a cultural one. The Conservatives tapped into a deep-seated desire for a return to national pride and traditional values, showing that culture, more than anything, is what drives political identity. As argued by Roger Scruton in *Where We Are*, people are inherently conservative as opposed to the Woke, cosmopolitan elites who deny the importance of community, family and national pride.

That very same electorate, feeling betrayed by the inaction of the Johnson (then Sunak) Government on those same values, retracted their votes from the Conservatives in 2024, preferring Nigel Farage's Reform Party, crippling the Tories primary vote and delivering a Starmer Labour Government their lowest poll since 2015. The Red Wall continues to grow in its discontent of the two-party establishment in Britain and is becoming the defining electorate in British politics.

Next, let's talk about Nicola Sturgeon and her spectacular fall from grace. Sturgeon, the former First Minister of Scotland, was riding high for nearly a decade, but her government's push for controversial transgender laws proved to be her undoing. The SNP's Gender Recognition Reform Bill aimed to make it easier for people to change their legal gender and facilitated biological men entering female prisons and changing rooms without any checks or balances. Unsurprisingly, the radical reforms faced significant opposition. And not just from the usual conservative suspects but also from feminists and the general Scottish public who were concerned about the impact on women's rights and safety. The backlash was fierce, and it exposed deep divisions within the SNP itself, ultimately leading to Sturgeon's resignation.

Then there are the farmers' protests in Europe. You see, while city-dwellers were busy sipping lattes and discussing the latest environmental policies, farmers across the continent were having none of it. In places like the Netherlands, France, and Germany they took to the streets, quite literally, to protest regulations that threatened their livelihoods. The Dutch government's plan to reduce nitrogen emissions by cutting livestock was the final straw, and farmers responded with a movement that quickly gained widespread support. This wasn't just about farming; it was about resisting what many see as an elite-driven agenda that ignores the needs of rural communities. The protests have fuelled the rise of populist movements that are sceptical of the EU's influence and critical of the disconnect between Brussels and ordinary citizens.

Finally, we have the rise of right-leaning parties across the EU including Italy's Brothers of Italy, Hungary's Fidesz, Poland's Law and Justice Party. These parties have gained ground by pushing back against the liberal, globalist consensus that has held sway in Europe for decades. They emphasise national sovereignty, traditional values, and a healthy dose of scepticism towards the EU's policies on immigration and social issues. In short, they're offering an alternative to the integrationist and progressive agendas that have dominated for so long, and they're finding a receptive audience among voters who feel left behind by the rapid social changes of recent years.

So, why does any of this matter? Well, for anyone looking to push back against Woke culture Europe's conservative resurgence offers some valuable lessons. First, it shows the importance of tapping into cultural identity and traditional values. People aren't just voting with their wallets; they're voting with their hearts, and that means understanding what they hold dear. Second, it highlights the dangers of pushing too far, too fast. As Sturgeon's fall shows, even the most powerful leaders can be toppled when they lose touch with the people they're supposed to represent.

For Australians, the takeaway is clear, don't underestimate the power of cultural issues in shaping political landscapes. The tide can turn quickly, and when it does, it's often because someone has finally decided to speak to the values that the average person holds dear. Whether it's resisting top-down environmental policies that ignore local needs or pushing back against radical social changes, the key is to mobilise and coordinate with rational fellow travellers. And if Europe's experience is anything to go by, there's plenty of room for a conservative resurgence Down Under too.

Ultimately, the culture wars will only see a decisive and conclusive victory when centre right governments make meaningful legislative changes that unravel the last twenty years of progressive mission creep. And there are several examples of this being done overseas.

Quietly and effectively, a conservative counterattack has been gathering steam across the globe, scoring some significant political and legislative victories. And make no mistake, these aren't just symbolic wins – they're reshaping the cultural and legal landscape in a way that's sending shockwaves through the bastions of Woke ideology. Let's take a closer look at what they did, how they did it, and why it matters for anyone looking to push back against the madness.

First off, let's talk about the Tavistock Centre in the UK. For years, this gender clinic was prescribing experimental hormone therapies to children and adolescents diagnosed with gender dysphoria. But after a series of damning reports and lawsuits, it became clear that things weren't quite as rosy as they seemed. Enter Dr. Hilary Cass, who led an enquiry that exposed some shocking practices, including the widespread use of puberty blockers without sufficient mental health assessments and a lack of alternative treatment options. The results were so damning that the UK government had no choice but to shut the place down and ban the use of puberty blockers for minors. This was a significant victory for vulnerable children and a major policy shift that emphasised caution, evidence-based medicine, and a return to common sense.

Meanwhile, across the pond in Florida, Governor Ron DeSantis has been busy making waves of his own. One of his biggest moves was the 'Parental Rights in Education' bill, which critics quickly dubbed the 'Don't Say Gay' bill. But what it really did was put the brakes on discussions of sexual orientation and gender identity in classrooms, particularly for younger students. DeSantis argued that parents, not schools, should have the final say in what their children are taught about these issues. It was a bold pushback against the indoctrination of children in progressive ideologies.

But DeSantis didn't stop there. He also took aim at the much-loved-by-degrowth-elites ESG (Environmental, Social, and Governance) principles, which have been creeping into every corner of the business world. DeSantis signed legislation prohibiting Florida's state fund managers from considering ESG factors in their investment decisions, arguing that these principles prioritise politics over profits. By positioning himself as a defender of economic freedom, DeSantis sent a clear message; Florida isn't going to be a playground for corporate virtue signalling.

And then, there's Donald Trump. Love him or hate him, you can't deny that his presidency left a lasting impact on the U.S. Supreme Court. Trump appointed three conservative justices, Neil Gorsuch, Brett Kavanaugh, and Amy Coney Barrett, who have shifted the Court's balance to the right. This new conservative majority has wasted no time in making its presence felt, especially on issues like free speech and abortion. Take the Masterpiece Cakeshop case, where the Court ruled in favour of a Christian baker who refused to make a wedding cake for a same-sex couple. Or the more recent Dobbs decision, which overturned Roe v. Wade and returned the power to regulate abortion to the states. These rulings are a testament to the enduring influence of Trump's judicial picks and represent significant victories for those who believe in limited government, black letter law and individual rights.

So, why does all of this matter for anyone looking to push back against Woke culture? Simple, these victories show that it's not just about making noise; it's about translating cultural resistance into concrete policy changes. Whether it's shutting down a controversial gender clinic, reforming education to give parents more control, or appointing judges who will defend the Constitution as it was written, these actions have real-world consequences. They prove that it's possible to push back against the progressive agenda and actually win.

For Australians looking for inspiration, the message is clear, don't just complain about the state of things, do something about it. Whether it's advocating for policy changes, supporting leaders who are willing to take a stand, or simply refusing to go along with the latest Woke fad, the key is to turn cultural resistance into tangible results. The battle is far from over, but these victories demonstrate that the conservative movement is capable of achieving meaningful change. The only question is, who's next? And if the Brits and Americans can do it, what's stopping Australians from doing the same?

It only takes a small, but vocal and well organised minority to shift a majority view. While that sounds a bit alarming, it's also a beacon of hope. By building our own networks and championing the values that have stood the test of time, like truth, beauty, liberty, and personal responsibility, we've got a shot at turning things around.

Let's face it, we're in the middle of a culture war, but up until now, it feels like only one side has been actively engaged in the fight. If we want truth and freedom to prevail, we've got to roll up our sleeves and start creating culture ourselves. That means making art, music, films, and content that reflect our values and inspire leadership. And then translating this cultural momentum into political outcomes. This groundwork will be essential if we're ever going to see the legislative and societal changes we desperately need.

Gerard Holland is the Executive Director Page Research Centre and was raised on a farm in Greenethorpe, NSW, he now lives in Bathurst with his wife and newborn son. Prior to joining Page, Gerard was the Director of Outreach and Strategic Partnerships at the Alliance for Responsible Citizenship in London and led the secretariat for the Legatum Institute's Transformation of Society programme. Whilst in London, he also advised as a speech writer for CEO Baroness Philippa Stroud.

Gerard has also worked as an electorate officer to former Regional Development and Communications Minister and Deputy Leader of the National Party, the Hon. Fiona Nash, and spent a season in Canada as a screenwriter.

Chapter Eight

THE EDUCATIONAL RENEWAL

From the outside and superficially it seems there is little to be optimistic about when it comes to education. In Australia, our politicised National Curriculum, declining PISA scores, gnashing of teeth over NAPLAN literacy and numeracy tests at years 3, 5, 7 and 9, increasing instances of school refusal, and numerous studies demonstrating the negative impacts of poor classroom behaviour, technology, and mental health, suggest we are in an educational nosedive with little chance of pulling up.

But not all is lost as across the Western world an educational renewal is underway committed to intellectual rigour, to clear thinking and truthful speaking, to immersing students in the best that has been thought and said throughout history, and that believes such a thing as 'the best' even exists at all. Quite possibly you have never heard of this renewal, as the media pays it scarce attention – and when it does, it is often to accuse it of racist or patriarchal motivations. Earlier chapters in this anthology detail why this is the case; that is, why the powers-that-be would make such denunciations. This chapter, on the other hand, is dedicated to describing this educational renewal, what undergirds it, and the positive impact it is having across the globe with a special focus on Australia.

Because it is community-based and not controlled by a top-down bureaucracy, this renewal looks different from city to city, country to country, and it goes under many names. Often it is known as either classical or liberal education, and unlike most government-sanctioned educational approaches, it unashamedly teaches the history of Western civilisation – both the good and the bad. The movement to recast education recognises as valuable approaches to education from as far back as Ancient Greece and Rome, through the Middle Ages and into the Enlightenment, this approach seeks to re-humanise what has been dehumanised in modern, progressive education.

From the earliest beginnings of the classical renewal in the American state of Idaho, this movement has grown to include thousands of schools across the world. Not only is its presence felt in primary and secondary schooling, but the tertiary space is likewise reconnecting with its original purpose, not merely for job preparation and credentialing, but for grounding young minds in a knowledge and love of history and literature and granting them the ability to reason logically and speak persuasively.

This chapter will summarise some of the renewal's major tenets and focus on a few particular examples from the United States, the United Kingdom, and Australia, with the aim to give the reader hope for an educational future that reverses the decline by rediscovering objective value, truth, beauty, and goodness; recommitting to educational excellence and intellectual rigour; reconnecting students to the wisdom of those that have gone before us; and reinstating true liberty as the heart of education.

To understand the nature of this renewal, it is important to recognise the distinction between K-12 schools and tertiary institutions. The description Classical Education is usually employed to describe K-12 schools, whereas Liberal Arts is more often associated with tertiary education; however, it is a concept that is included within the classical paradigm. While these words and concepts are laden with historical definitions, over time they have come to be redefined in ways that are not necessarily congruent with their initial intent.

Historically speaking, the Liberal Arts denoted the course of study for the liberated man. Finding their foundation in Ancient Greece, and then being codified in Latin medievalism, the Seven Liberal Arts consisted of the Trivium of Grammar, Logic, and Rhetoric which comprise the three language arts, and the Quadrivium of Arithmetic, Geometry, Astronomy, and Music – the mathematical arts. Instruction in these disciplines formed the foundation of Western education for over a thousand years. This is why the classical education movement incorporates the Liberal Arts; these were the arts that formed the foundation of a classical education, where classical refers specifically to Ancient Greece and Rome.

Classical Education in K-12 schools is an approach grounded in classical pedagogy and curriculum, including the Trivium and Quadrivium. But, as the name suggests, it also places a heavy focus on Western history, by teaching such authors as Homer, Virgil, Sophocles, Dante, and Shakespeare, as well as classical philosophy. Very often, these schools will also teach either Latin or Greek. This focus on history also informs how subjects are taught, such as through Socratic discussions and mimetic instruction, with a heavy focus on grammar and logic. There is also an explicit emphasis on character development in classical schools, many of which purposefully aim at forming intellectual and moral virtues in students so that they're prepared not only to be good future workers, but also – and more importantly – to be good people and good citizens.

While classical schools often teach the Seven Liberal Arts as subjects, some also employ the Trivium as a process of determining stages of pedagogical approaches. In 1947 Dorothy Sayers wrote the essay 'The Lost Tools of Learning' which became instrumental in revivifying the classical approach. Under this schema, the stages of childhood development are coded to the three parts of the Trivium: grammar is the early stage from pre-school to around ten years old, logic is for students around ten to fourteen, and the rhetoric stage is for the upper years of secondary school. Each of these stages has a different focus: grammar is about filling young minds with knowledge (a similar approach to that of E.D. Hirsch. Jr which is discussed below), logic introduces dialectical thinking where students ask and are asked more complex questions and work through systems of logical and critical thinking, and rhetoric teaches students to combine these areas and express themselves clearly, persuasively and thoroughly.

In many ways classical education is just good old-fashioned quality schooling. As a case in point, a resurgence in evidence-led educational practice is currently sweeping Australia, typified by a phonics and phonemic awareness approach to reading and the importance of direct instruction. This move is in reaction to the last 50 years of Australian education having been dominated by a whole-language approach to reading and a student-led, project-based, inquiry approach to learning.

This is the consistent story of modern progressive education – new fads and techniques are pushed into schools, often poorly evidenced, and a generation of students suffer as a result. But phonics and phonemic awareness and direct instruction have always been and will always be hallmarks of classical education. Because it is grounded in history, tradition, and tried and tested methods, it does not get caught up in every apparently groundbreaking piece of technology or radical new approach to education, and thus does not suffer from the constant whiplash with which teachers in most schools are sadly familiar.

While similar to what is happening in school education, in colleges and universities a Liberal Arts education has come to mean something more like an education in the humanities with Western civilisation as the curriculum cornerstone. Rather than teaching the Seven Liberal Arts themselves, these colleges often teach the core humanities subjects of literature, history, philosophy, and theology. This is akin to the liberal education of the Enlightenment and is the kind of undergraduate education that most university students would have received until the vocation-specific specialisation and credentialing approach that has dominated the last century.

What these schools and colleges share is a respect for Western civilisation and the Judaeo-Christian heritage that has shaped our world today. They shirk modern, new-age progressive approaches to education, recognising the value of knowledge of history, an appreciation of great books, the ability to think and reason logically, and, for many of them, a firm foundation in theology as the 'queen of the sciences'. Such schools also promote independent critical thinking based on rationality and reason instead of cultural-left mind control and group think.

Before identifying some noteworthy examples, it is worth commenting on the word 'liberal'. What does it mean for an education to be liberal? The ancients purposefully delineated it from the servile arts, which were those committed to specifically utilitarian ends, whereas the liberal arts were those for the liberated man, the man free to pursue the life of the mind. While still a worthy definition, over time it has come to mean more than that. I would suggest that the liberal arts are not only *for* the liberated human, but they are also part of the liberating process. A liberal education is an education which sets one free. Of course, this implies that people are in some way captive, and here Plato's 'Allegory of the Cave' is instructional. To summarise it briefly: in a subterranean cave people are chained and forced to face a wall on which shadows are projected. For these cave-dwellers, the two-dimensional images are the sum totality of reality. However, once freed, they can move above ground and in the light of the sun experience true reality, knowledge and understanding.

Liberal education brings people out of the captivity of their own ignorance, out of their favoured echo-chambers, out of the temporal biases of their present, out of their unexamined cultural assumptions; and importantly, out of the dominating narratives pushed by external powers like the media, their friends and colleagues, the academic elite, and political authorities. Liberal education, by liberating the mind from the small world of the imminent and present, and revealing the history of the world, the greatest ideas from the greatest minds, and the true, the good and beautiful, frees the individual to see reality as it really is.

Apart from the gifts of objectivity and rationality that classical liberal education bestows, importantly, it also produces excellent results. As the movement grows, the evidence is stacking up to prove that its students surpass the academic standards of all other mainstream sectors of education. One of the most thorough longitudinal pieces of research recently conducted is the *Good Soil Report* which demonstrated that not only were classical educated students well above the national averages in grades and college achievement, but also measured other important results like participation in civic life, and time spent volunteering in their community.

The Good Soil Report was prepared by the Association of Classical Christian Schools (ACCS), which is the largest advocacy organisation for classical Christian education in the United States, representing over 470 schools across the nation. Its main goals are to advocate for classical Christian education, to support and offer accreditation to schools, and to equip teachers and administration to be able to provide high quality education. While there are many tangible metrics demonstrating the movement's results, to single one out, in 2019, the average ACCS student's score on the Scholastic Aptitude Test was 1246, compared to the national average of 1059; for Australian comparison, that is roughly the difference between an ATAR of 77 and 87.

The Catholic alternative to the ACCS is the Institute for Catholic Liberal Education. The ICLE represents 240 schools and expresses its mission as "drawing on the Church's tradition of education, which frees teachers and students for the joyful pursuit of faith, wisdom, and virtue". While ICLE schools are part of the classical renewal, they purposefully chose to employ the term liberal to draw attention to the liberating propensity of true education. A large part of ICLE's approach is in the renewal of small, often struggling, Catholic schools, helping them to rediscover what was, as their website states, the "gold standard of formation for centuries". An example is St Jerome Academy in Maryland, which went from barely surviving with dwindling numbers and unreconcilable debt, to almost doubling in size with a waiting list of over 120 students by adopting the classical approach. Within this Catholic sector is a smaller but growing organisation called the Chesterton Schools Network. Founded in 2007, Chesterton schools all follow the same curriculum involving literature, history, philosophy, theology, and foreign language, anchored to historical periods in each year level. Along with this, students study science and maths including astronomy and Euclidian geometry, and the fine arts including music and art history. While their schools are primarily located in the United States, more and more are emerging across the world, including in Europe and Africa.

Another significant approach to quality education within the United

States is through the Charter School program. Great Hearts Academies manage over forty schools offering a classical liberal arts education. As stated on their website, they believe that a "liberal education consists of cognitive, emotional, and moral education – thinking deeply, loving noble things, and living well together. [They] believe, with Plato, that the highest goal of education is to become good, intellectually and morally". Tuition for Great Hearts is free, and they have worked to create opportunities for more than just those that have a local school by moving their program online, which helps to explain how they cater for over 25,000 students.

This is just one example of the way parents who care about quality education for their children can use technology to avoid the pitfalls of the current educational system to access the kind of schooling that all students deserve. Technology can help to democratise schooling and de-monopolise it from governmental control. Unlike other organisations, Great Hearts Academies are non-religious, demonstrating that the liberal and classical ideal is not strictly bound to the Christian faith. As part of their rigorous liberal curriculum, the Academies focus on core foundational knowledge when teaching history and geography, and they do so by implementing another program that deserves mention, The Core Knowledge Foundation.

Lest the renewal as outlined above suggests that emerging approaches to good quality education are mainly classical or mainly religious, it is important to note that liberal education goes beyond these limits. One approach that aligns to liberal principles and has been steadily growing in popularity is the Core Knowledge Foundation, based on the work of Professor E.D. Hirsch. Jr. Since publishing his book *Cultural Literacy* in 1987, Hirsch has become known as a proponent of the importance of knowledge as the foundation of a student's learning. Without core knowledge upon which to build and anchor new knowledge as well as skills such as critical thinking, students are cast adrift, often asked to consider questions that make sense to educated adults but are meaningless to those without the prerequisite knowledge base.

Over the recent decades, Australia has fallen for the allure of introducing critical thinking into schools as early as possible. However, as Hirsch and others such as Daniel Willingham have demonstrated for over forty years, while students have a natural proclivity for problem solving this does not necessarily suggest they should be fed exclusively or even significantly on this type of learning; in fact, it might even suggest the opposite. And secondly, while critical thinking skills are vital, it is impossible to think critically until we have knowledge to think critically *about*, hence the importance of what Hirsch calls "Core Knowledge".

In the prologue to his 2016 book *Knowledge Matters*, he summarises the rapid decline of French public schooling when, in 1989, it moved from teaching all French students a core cultural knowledge base, towards an individualised, child-centred and skills focused curriculum. Within ten years of this change, the French schooling system was widely regarded as being in crisis. Part of this crisis is the lack of cultural literacy; the core knowledge previously provided that inducted French students into French culture and history, helped them to appreciate their debt to the West, and gifted them their inheritance of its cultural patrimony. This is a major characteristic of liberal education that provides a stark contrast between it and Woke, progressive education that so often demeans, dismisses and demonises Western civilisation's heritage.

The Core Knowledge foundation stresses the fundamental importance of knowledge based upon the following principles: knowledge builds on knowledge; knowledge is the key to reading comprehension; shared knowledge makes communication possible; and equal access to knowledge promotes excellence and fairness. This movement has been embraced in over six hundred schools across the United States, and increasingly popular across the world in countries as diverse as New Zealand, the UAE, Peru, Cambodia and the U.K.

One of these schools is the United Kingdom's Michaela Community School. If you are at all interested in education, it is likely that you have heard of Michaela, run by Katharine Birbalsingh, who is sometimes referred to as 'Britain's strictest headteacher'. Birbalsingh is a supporter of E.D. Hirch Jr's work, and as such, Michaela focuses on knowledge as the core of learning. Along with this, though, the school has a traditional approach to teaching including direct instruction, call and response, and learning knowledge by rote. It is important to note that Michaela is in a significantly underprivileged area where one-third of households are living in poverty, and its student-body includes a high percentage of diverse racial and religious minority groups.

Despite this, the results speak for themselves. In 2019, 18% of Michaela's students received the highest possible grade on their GCSEs, compared to the national average of 4.5%. In 2024, 93% of its students received above a Grade 5 in GSCE English and maths, compared to a 45% national average. As such, Birbalsingh has become an internationally sought after keynote speaker, and was appointed Commander of the Order of British Empire in 2020. Despite this success, and perhaps unsurprisingly, the school has consistent denigrators. The use of traditional curriculum and pedagogy, strict rules, and a focus on unity where individual licence is sacrificed for the good of the group, means that progressives simply cannot accept that the triumph is worth the apparent cost. Birbalsingh's recognition that individuals often need to sacrifice some personal freedoms in the name of 'Britishness' is a difficult pill to swallow for those who don't believe in 'Britishness' and think they're advocating for the downtrodden. However, as Michaela's results consistently demonstrate, the best way to advocate for the downtrodden is to give them access to high quality education.

Moving from the K-12 space to the tertiary, it is not only primary and secondary education that has suffered at the hands of Woke ideologues resulting in a decline in not only standards, but a complete shift in the rationale for the institution's existence. One university that is purposefully attempting to return to the traditional *raison d'etre* of tertiary education opened its doors in late 2024. The University of Austin (UATX) describes itself as being dedicated to the "fearless pursuit of the truth", recognising that "others have abandoned this core mission of the university".

With a board of trustees that includes Bari Weiss and Niall Ferguson, and a board of advisors including Jonathon Haidt, Richard Dawkins, and Ayaan Hirsi Ali, its philosophy is clear. It is early days for UATX, but that the need for such an institution exists, and that it explains its mission in such specific language exemplifies not only the decay in the sector, but also the way out of it. The founding president of the University is Dr Pano Kanelos, who was previously the President of another American institution worth mentioning, St John's College, Annapolis.

St John's is widely acknowledged as the foremost Great Books college in the world. With a history that dates back to 1696, St John's, like Campion College in Australia, focuses its attention primarily on one degree – a bachelor's degree in liberal arts. It follows the Great Books Program developed in the 1930s by a number of academics, including Mortimer Adler, who also formulated a pedagogical approach for K-12 schools called the *Paideia* Program, which is often utilised in classical classrooms. The program at St John's exposes students to what is sometimes referred to as the great conversation of great ideas throughout history, including works in theology, literature, music, politics, mathematics, science and poetry. So renowned as a bastion of liberal education is St John's that it was selected as the premier institution for Australian students awarded postgraduate scholarships by the Ramsay Centre for Western Civilisation.

The Ramsay Centre brings us back to Australia, where, though the renewal has been underway internationally for decades, it is still in its very early stages. At the time of writing there is a small number of schools that are in some way informed by the classical liberal tradition. All of the schools are at different stages of their journey, ranging from seeking accreditation to fully operating.

Among schools that are operational, two examples of the way forward are Toowoomba Christian College (TCC) and Brisbane's St John of Kronstadt Academy (SJKA). TCC describes itself as a Christian School in the Liberal Arts Tradition. It purposefully avoids the 'classical' moniker to avoid assumptions about how closely it will align to the American style of classical education. The school was founded in 1979, but it wasn't until around 2017 that the decision was made to adopt the liberal arts approach. As such, the transition has been purposefully measured and gradual to account for the lack of awareness in the community as to what the liberal arts tradition is. As a school of 800 students P-12, it is the largest intentionally liberal arts school in Australia, and while it has a long way to go, it is possibly the furthest along the journey of implementing what this kind of education could look like in Australia.

On the other end of the size spectrum, St John of Kronstadt Academy opened for students in Prep to Year 3 in January 2024. The Academy is thoroughly classical, drawing consistently upon the U.S. model of classical Christian education. It is the first of its kind in Australia, not only as a Russian Orthodox classical school, but, to my knowledge, the first school designed and intended from the outset specifically as a classical school. Other schools that are either informed by or implementing a classical liberal approach include, but are not limited to, Hartford College in Sydney, Covenant Christian School in Canberra, St Philomena's in Park Ridge, St Theodore's of Canterbury in Perth, and St Benedict School in Adelaide Hills. In Western Australia, The Classical School and Coram Deo offer hybrid micro-schooling options that are possible due to the state's home-schooling regulations. It is also interesting to note that in 2023 one of the oldest schools in Australia, St Mary's Cathedral College in Sydney started using language signifying a move towards a liberal arts approach to pedagogy.

Despite the recent activity taking place in the K-12 schools, within Australia over the past few decades the most consistent voice advocating for and providing a liberal arts education has been Campion College in Sydney. Opened in 2006, Campion is Australia's first liberal arts tertiary college. Now boasting over 300 alumni who work in industries including education, journalism, business, law, medicine, and politics, Campion has long been at the forefront of liberal education in Australia. In addition to this, the recently established Ramsay Centre undergraduate programs of Western Civilisation at the University of

Queensland, the University of Wollongong, and the Australian Catholic University, mean that the value of a liberal education in universities and colleges is once again starting to be recognised.

The final school to mention is St John Henry Newman College (SJHNC). Planning to commence teaching in 2026, SJHNC is an independent Catholic classical school in Brisbane, of which I am honoured to be the founding principal. My work in this space over the last decade has proven to me that much more is possible in the Australian educational space than is first apparent. While we have the National Curriculum that must form the basis of programs in all schools, it is broad enough that a classical liberal education is very much achievable within its confines. Such is the program that will be delivered at SJHNC. Students will be immersed in the true, good, and beautiful through the reading of great books, learning Latin, enjoying music and the arts, and an approach to learning that utilises tried and tested methods of rote-learning, direct instruction, phonics, phonemic awareness and grammar, as well as relegating technology to where is it actually useful and needed, as opposed to placing it at the centre of all classrooms which is so often the case in contemporary Australian schools.

There is an additional element that the classical liberal approach provides that is perhaps more needed now than at any other time in human history. At the outset of this chapter, I outlined some of the issues plaguing Australian education, and amongst them were school refusal and declining mental health. While not a silver bullet, this traditional approach to education provides something to young minds and souls which is often sorely lacking: meaning. An education in reality brings people out of the captivity of their own minds and into the light of beauty and truth.

As such, and particularly when it is anchored in the Christian faith, classical education contributes to the remedy for the meaning-crisis that is facing the West. Rather than a form of choose-your-own-adventure relativistic existentialism that flattens reality and robs it of purpose in the name of tolerance and acceptance, an education in the liberal arts includes young people in a story of meaning found through responsibility. It is the natural home for an education that truly deals with the "whole child", including the spiritual and transcendent in the everyday activities of the classroom.

While there are unmistakable issues with the West's education system, there is a growing flame of a renewal. This renewal is first and foremost one of high-quality education. Classical liberal education provides the foundation needed for all students to enter adult life not narrowly suited to just one particular career, and not so ideologically indoctrinated that they can no longer see logic or common sense. Rather, this is a true education that liberates students to see reality rightly and to respond to it accordingly. Truth should be at the heart of education and if we focus on a deep knowledge of history, a love of great literature and art, a mind trained in logical mathematical and scientific thinking, an appreciation of tradition and the sacrifices of those that have come before us, the formation of wisdom and virtue, and an acceptance of personal accountability and responsibility, then it is possible to correct our path and reverse the decline.

Kenneth (Diff) Crowther is the founding principal of Brisbane's St John Henry Newman College and has worked as an educator for over fifteen years, teaching in the fields of literature, history, and philosophy. He writes and speaks regularly about the burgeoning classical liberal education movement in Australia and has co-hosted the 'Educating Humans' podcast about this topic since 2022. From Macquarie University he holds Master of Arts, and from the University of Southern Queensland, a Bachelor of Arts and Education, a Master of Arts, and a current PhD candidature with a focus on Early Modern English theatre and culture.

Chapter Nine

THE TIDE IS TURNING – AUSTRALIA AND THE INDIGENOUS VOICE TO PARLIAMENT

Western culture is increasingly copping a bashing from highly vocal people who have been influenced by cultural-left ideology. I don't know what proportion of people embrace this ideology, but I do know that they seem to have a huge collective voice, and, as such, disproportionate influence. The aim of this anthology is to demonstrate that while Western culture is less than perfect, there is significant pushback from concerned people who believe that we have a lot to be grateful for from what Western culture offers. This pushback has resulted in a major ideological battle, one that is relevant for all Australians. In this chapter, I focus on this battle as it relates to Aboriginal Australians and, by implication, all Australians. There is perhaps no other group of Australians, namely Aboriginal Australians, about whom it is claimed that they, more than any other group, have suffered and continue to suffer from the impact of Western culture.

While I acknowledge the role of British settlement in disrupting Aboriginal people's way of life initially, I do not believe that Western culture is the *cause* of suffering among Aboriginal people *today*. But many disagree, hence the ideological battle we have. As a result, today, we have schools teaching their students to apologise for colonisation, corporations rolling out cultural awareness programs, and governments producing anti-racism campaigns. In addition, we have programs that have Aboriginal people taking visits 'on country' as a means for healing or other initiatives that claim to connect them with their Aboriginal culture. This would all be fine if it resulted in any practical benefit to Aboriginal people, but I see little evidence of this. The failure of these practices to yield practical benefits suggests to me that the assumed cause of Aboriginal suffering is inaccurate; that is, Aboriginal people today are not suffering as a result of Western culture.

Rather than framing Western culture as the cause of problems facing Aboriginal Australians today, I believe it is fair to suggest that much of the suffering and disadvantage results from inadequate access to the material benefits Western culture has to offer. It is worth mentioning that governments and Aboriginal leaders have a key role to play here in ensuring that Aboriginal Australians have access to the same opportunities and benefits that most other Australians take for granted.

Last year, in 2023, we saw a national reckoning of Aboriginal issues; arguably the most defining in recent times. Although the Voice to Parliament referendum did not explicitly state that Western culture was the culprit affecting Aboriginal Australians, it was surely implied, given that the Voice proposal was premised on the idea that they lack a Voice in mainstream society – society which is underpinned by Western culture's institutions, ideas, practices, and values. In this chapter I discuss the referendum, its reason for being proposed, why it had appeal initially, and why the Australian voting public eventually went against the tide.

In seeking to understand why there was a volte-face, I look at some external factors like the role of conservative campaigners such as Advance Australia, major right-wing think tanks, and prominent Aboriginal leaders. Combined, they delivered a message which, in essence, stated that the Voice was not the way to go. I also consider some internal factors like the psyche of the Australian voting public, to try and understand what impact pro-Voice messages from celebrities and corporations had on their thinking. Finally, I discuss where to now, given that the referendum is over, because although this battle has ended, the war is far from over. By that, I mean that there are many people who still think that Western culture is the underlying cause of problems facing Aboriginal people, and hence, will use Voice-like mechanisms in the belief that these will help Aboriginal Australians.

There is little doubt that Aboriginal Australians are the most disadvantaged group of Australians in regard to health and general wellbeing. A common explanation for this inequity, as already mentioned, is the negative impact of Western culture. Undeniably, the British arrival (or 'invasion' if you prefer), with its Western culture, resulted in a great loss of Aboriginal lives and a catastrophic disruption to their way of life. Under Western culture, Aboriginal people were regularly seen as 'not equals', and their culture was neither understood nor appreciated. It is understandable, then, that some see Western culture and values as the culprits holding Aboriginal people back today

Some 200 years after colonisation, we are faced with the question "To what extent is the current disadvantage faced by Aboriginal Australians today attributable to Western culture?". Those who advocated for the Voice clearly believed the past is highly relevant in explaining the problems facing Aboriginal Australians today. In an article on *The Guardian* webpage entitled 'Historians urge Australians to "be on the right side of history" when they vote in voice referendum', its author states "The 'historic injustices' suffered by Indigenous Australians warrant a voice to parliament, according to hundreds of historians, with a new public campaign calling on voters to consider the nation's colonial past when casting their ballot".

This claim contained in *The Guardian* fails to recognise that many Aboriginal Australians are doing exceedingly well by conventional measures of success and therefore, seem well adjusted to Western culture in the main. Hence, I do not believe that historical injustices (i.e., colonisation) are the cause of suffering among those Aboriginal Australians today. However, while many Aboriginal people are doing well and some are doing exceedingly well, there are far too many who are suffering, so it is natural to ask why the health and wellbeing statistics for Aboriginal Australians are so concerning?

I will answer this question in the next section. There were two main drivers for the call for the 2023 Voice to Parliament referendum. The first was the belief that some form of official recognition of Aboriginal people was needed. Much of the voting public would not object to this.

The second driver was the belief that current and successive governments were not capable of fully understanding the needs of Aboriginal Australians. On this last point, the Voice was promoted as a 'game changer' because it was assumed it would be better able to harness Aboriginal values, skills, and knowledge, resulting in Aboriginal-guided solutions that would ultimately lead to improved health and wellbeing. Voice proponents typically believed this poorer health and wellbeing is directly or indirectly the result of Western culture. Western culture, the dominant culture in Australia, is often portrayed by 'blactivists' as dismissive of Aboriginal culture, sometimes oppressive and racist, and a culture which is not conducive for Aboriginal Australians to thrive. Hence, it was assumed that a Voice to Parliament would address this.

However, I believe that casting Western culture as the problem, and hence Aboriginal culture as the solution, is part of a flawed ideology that is not new. It is just the latest incarnation of the same ideology that has dominated Aboriginal affairs for as long as I can remember. The ideology I refer to is best expressed as a set of related ideas: that Aboriginal Australians continue to suffer due to the assumed ongoing effects of colonisation; Australia as a country is racist against Aboriginal Australians; Aboriginal Australians have needs that are fundamentally different from other Australians; Aboriginal Australians possess a culture that is distinct from and largely incompatible with Australia's Westernised culture; and it is infinitely preferable that Aboriginal Australians be the ones to help Aboriginal Australians. Stated more succinctly, Aboriginal culture is the solution to the problem of Western culture that adversely impacts on Aboriginal people.

I have seen this faulty ideology dominate, particularly in recent times, as more and more Australians embrace identity politics, political correctness, and virtue signalling (the evil trio). I believe that this ideology is the main reason why so many Aboriginal people still suffer so much. Overturn this ideology, and more Aboriginal Australians will be able to access the sorts of opportunities and modern services that most non-Aboriginal Australians take for granted. Understand that Aboriginal Australians have the same fundamental needs as non-Aboriginal Australians, and proposed solutions will be more effective.

Given the widespread acceptance of this Woke ideology, I initially expected that the Voice referendum result would be a resounding Yes. And certainly, the early polls seemed to confirm this. We heard emotional pleas from the Prime Minister, telling us that a Yes vote in the Voice to Parliament referendum is a "once in a generation chance" for Australians. When I saw academics, celebrities, Indigenous peak bodies, well-respected Aboriginal leaders, and corporates urging us to vote Yes, I thought a Yes outcome was all but guaranteed. But despite optimistic polling and efforts by the Yes team, Australia voted No to the Voice, 60% to 40%.

A month before the referendum, I wrote in *The Australian* newspaper that if the Voice wins, it will be won on emotion. Let me explain. The American psychologist Jonathan Haidt has said "The emotional tail wags the rational dog". He is saying that we often make decisions based more on emotion than rationality and reason. Emotions are fine when used in partnership with rational thought. I believe that in the early days of the Voice referendum campaigning, the Yes message appealed strongly to the emotions.

Most Australians are aware that Aboriginal people do far poorer on a range of health and wellbeing indicators. And not only do they wish that this was not the case, but they also want only the best for Aboriginal Australians. This regrettable state of poorer health, education and wellbeing certainly stirs their emotions. In addition, even if they do not know any Aboriginal people themselves, they often see in the media the plight of Aboriginal Australians, so Aboriginal people are not out of sight and very much on the minds of a sympathetic public.

While being very concerned about Aboriginals, perhaps Aussies also feel frustrated at not being able to do anything themselves to help Aboriginal Australians. Perhaps they even feel a little bit of guilt? Feelings of frustration and guilt are not pleasant. But then the Voice was proposed as a solution to the problems facing Aboriginal people.

According to then Minister for Indigenous Australians, Linda Burney, as quoted on an ABC webpage, the Voice would be "nimble, efficient and focused on making a practical difference". Vote Yes and not only will your feelings of shame and guilt vanish but you will be on the right side of history. How good is that!

A very emotive topic is that of racism. While I do not believe the Yes camp used claims of racism as a key strategy to persuade voters, there were subtle and not-so-subtle hints that a No vote was tied to racism. Consider the words of Professor Marcia Langton "The No campaign is using racism to peddle their deceitful wares". Or consider the words of journalist Niki Savva, who, while not explicit in her claim that a No vote was an expression of racism, stated "While it is not true to say that every Australian who votes no in the Voice referendum is a racist, you can bet your bottom dollar that every racist will vote no". If there was any truth to Savva's words, then it was likely because a No vote was promoted by the Yes team as being harmful to Aboriginal Australians (i.e., depriving them of having a say on Aboriginal affairs). Naturally, a No vote would then be attractive to racists.

So, while Australians were not explicitly branded as racist in the lead up to the referendum, after failing to achieve the much-desired Yes outcome, some prominent figures have since expressed their view that rejecting the Voice proposal was associated with racism (or a dislike of Aboriginal Australians). Consider the following claims made after the Voice referendum:

> Quoting from an ABC webpage "Reconciliation Victoria acting co-chair, Emily Poelina-Hunter, a Nyikina woman, was not surprised by the findings of the (human rights commission) report after the 'devastating year of racism' last year following the Voice referendum results".

The Australian newspaper reported that the prominent Voice architect, Megan Davis said in her NAIDOC Week keynote lecture delivered at the University of Queensland that the failure to include Aboriginal Australians in the Constitution implies they are somehow unimportant and that Aboriginal children returned to school on Monday after the referendum "feeling like they didn't belong".

Again, on an ABC webpage, 'Aunty' Lynette Riley was quoted as saying, "One of the things we saw as part of the debacle of the referendum was that Australia is still not proud of Aboriginal people".

Consider the words of ABC Indigenous affairs reporter Bridget Brennan, as quoted in *The Australian*, "When there is so much racism embedded in this country … (during the Voice) it was really horrible as an Aboriginal person … We know what exists in Australian society, we see it every day".

People generally do not wish to be called racist or associated with anything that is racist or could be construed as racist. Hence, this could partly explain why many people initially intended to vote Yes.

Of course, claims that Australians are racist against Aboriginal people did not just start with the Voice. For many decades it has been a national pastime to accuse non-indigenous Australians of being racist against Aboriginal people. For example, consider that when a *Closing the Gap* report is released, or there is an Aboriginal death in custody, or disturbing statistics on out-of-home care for Aboriginal children are given, claims that Australia is racist to Aboriginal Australians abound.

Initially, many Australians sincerely believed that when voting for the Voice referendum they were voting on whether they wanted to end the disproportionate suffering of Aboriginal Australians. I do not know of any voter who wouldn't vote Yes to this. Although it was unclear how the Voice would help Aboriginal Australians, in the early days, people didn't feel the need to know. The thought that a solution was being offered that promised to help Aboriginal Australians was enough to cause excitement, leading to a Yes vote. However, the referendum question was *not* asking people if they wanted to end the suffering of Aboriginal Australians. The question was "A Proposed Law: to alter the Constitution to recognise the First Peoples of Australia by establishing an Aboriginal and Torres Strait Islander voice. Do you approve this proposed alteration?".

As October 14 drew closer, both the Yes and No teams were doing their best to inform the public of what they believed the Voice was and was not. As people became more aware of what the referendum question was asking, they wanted to know how this Voice proposal would help Aboriginal people in practical ways. Statements like "A First Nations Voice will improve the lives of First Nations Peoples" on the Uluru Statement page were offered, but these were simply that, a statement and not an explanation.

On June 23, *The Conversation* published an article that aimed to convince the voting public that the Voice was the way to help Aboriginal Australians (not wanting to miss out on being on the right side of history, the University of NSW later published this article on their webpage). The article's authors posed the question "How will the Voice make a practical difference?" and provided the following answer, "The Voice will give Aboriginal and Torres Strait Islander people a constitutionally guaranteed right to speak to government and the parliament about what's needed for practical improvements to people's lives. This, in turn, would help address disadvantage and systemic discrimination".

But the public already knew that there was a Minister for Indigenous Australians and countless advisors and organisations dedicated to helping Aboriginal people. So, knowing that Aboriginal people already had their voices but were told they lacked them would have raised doubt in the minds of Yes voters. This is where leadership was important. Those leading the Yes campaign needed to reassure the people that their initial excitement was justified.

In June 2023, Prime Minister Anthony Albanese appeared on Channel 10's *The Project*, a place I would have thought was very safe for a Labor PM. The transcript is available from the PM's webpage (pm. gov.au). I give credit to the interviewers who weren't after any 'gotcha moments' but were asking reasonable questions. Consider this one from host Sam Taunton "Albo, I think I'm more across the arguments for the Voice more than most people because I work in this job, I'm consuming the news. But even I still don't really don't understand a lot of it. Do you get how confusing this is for most people?". Mr Albanese's response, in my opinion, did not provide clarity on how the Voice would work and what it would achieve.

Now consider in July 2023, the *ABC Insiders*, another Labor-friendly place, when host David Speers interviewed Indigenous Australians Minister Linda Burney. The transcript is available from the Department of the Prime Minister and Cabinet's webpage (ministers. pmc.gov.au). Again, with no gotcha moments, David Speers politely set about to find out from Linda Burney how the Voice would work. He respectfully asked "I'm just trying to get a sense for the viewers of how this works. If the Voice gets up at the referendum, would you, as Minister, be advising the Voice on what they should be advising you on?", yet she struggled to answer.

The fact that the Yes team, most notably senior leaders such as Anthony Albanese and Linda Burney, had not been able to communicate to the public what the Voice was and how it would benefit Aboriginal Australians, I believe, resulted in many Yes voters converting to the No vote.

On the night of the most recent federal election Mr Albanese stated in his victory speech that, "I commit to the Uluru Statement from the heart in full". What exactly did "in full" mean? I guess it depends on who you ask. But it would seem to involve some level of truth-telling and discussion about treaties. For many people, they were starting to think there was more to the Voice than just a "permanent advisory body that would give advice to the government about the issues that affect First Nations peoples" as described on the Uluru Statement webpage. Further adding to people's concerns was that a process that had not been well explained would involve changing our Constitution. This was a major concern because once the Constitution was modified to accommodate the Voice, it could not be easily changed back if it did not work. While many people were not certain about what the change to the Constitution would mean, they were certain that a change would be difficult to undo once made.

Psychology, as well as common sense, tells us humans have the fundamental need for some control over their lives. This need, commonly referred to as autonomy or agency, requires that we are able to make our decisions, free of external control, influence, coercion, and manipulation. When a person's autonomy is taken away from them or thwarted, they do not fare well. While it is true that people were ostensibly free to decide what box they would tick at the polls on referendum day, it would have been possible to influence them in a particular direction. Perhaps the many corporate and celebrity endorsements had some value in the early days in convincing people that the Yes vote was the right choice. However, it was clear that, in the end, quite a number of people resented the idea of their 'betters' telling them how to vote. Consequently, some Yes voters may have started to use their heads more than their hearts to conclude that the Voice proposal was not a good idea.

Right-wing think tanks (e.g., Centre for Independent Studies and Institute for Public Affairs) played a key role in providing public forums where the pros and cons of the Voice could be openly discussed. Not only were they highly active in the lead up to the referendum, but for several years prior, they had been promoting the virtues of Western culture, as well as providing specific and effective strategies for promoting the health and wellbeing of Aboriginal Australians. In addition, Advance Australia, an organisation committed to challenging Woke political leaders and elites, was especially active in equipping the public with excellent resource material highlighting problems with the Voice. Collectively, these organisations let the public know that there is a lot in Western culture to be grateful for.

However, while these organisations were able to convince people that voting No was good, they could still be subjected to peer pressure and criticism from Yes voters. People intending to vote No, needed credible people they could connect and identify with. Enter Jacinta Nampijinpa Price and Warren Mundine. Both these leaders had been publicly declaring for many years what needs to happen in order to close the gap, namely, a focus on community safety, access to education and jobs, and economic development. Most importantly, they let voters know that all of this can happen without the proposed Voice.

These two credible Aboriginal leaders, with their track records of going against the grain and rubbing shoulders with Aboriginal people in the boardrooms, the streets, and the dirt, were able to instil in those who lacked confidence, a conviction to unashamedly vote No. This conviction likely had a ripple effect where more of the voting public saw more people who were confident to declare to others that they were No voters. Subsequently, as the referendum drew closer, No voters stopped feeling ostracised. And clearly, the ripple turned into a flood.

The No victory essentially means that the government can now more freely focus on solutions that are known to help Aboriginal Australians lead healthy and fulfilling lives, such as education, employment, and community development. However, the defeat of the Voice does not automatically mean that the government of the day will implement these solutions. While the Voice has come to an end, its spirit continues through Woke leaders. As long as these leaders influence Aboriginal affairs, media, academia, and public perceptions, the challenges faced by Aboriginal Australians will continue to be attributed to racism, colonisation, cultural insensitivity, and the failings of Western culture. Defeating the Voice is a good start, but we must not stop there. We must continue to focus on the solutions known to work.

When I look at the Aboriginal leaders of the Yes team, I see that many have achieved great success in their chosen careers; some are recognised as great leaders of this country. Of course, the same can be said of the Aboriginal leaders of the No team, Jacinta Nampijinpa Price and Warren Mundine. They have done well in terms of mainstream society, while still strongly identifying as Aboriginal.

These Aboriginal leaders are proof that future generations of Aboriginal Australians can lead a fulfilling life, enjoying the many benefits that Western culture offers today and not be distracted by Woke sideshows.

Certainly, our Western culture contains much that is not good. However, as humans, we can and do make good decisions, choosing from the best that Western culture has to offer and opposing the not-so-good, and where appropriate, eliminating it. Finally, for those

Aboriginal people for whom it is important, I am not suggesting you need to abandon all elements of what you consider to be Aboriginal culture. By all means, take from it what you value. But it should be no surprise that there is some overlap between Aboriginal and Western cultures. One good aspect of Western culture, particularly in the Australian context, is that it accommodates multiple cultures. These cultures coexist and thrive in a balanced way when the values of basic goodness, a fair go, respect for others, caring for family, and mateship are valued.

Anthony Dillon is originally from Queensland, Anthony is proud of both his Aboriginal and non-Aboriginal ancestry, he has been an active social commentator on Aboriginal issues, for two decades. He has had several thought-provoking articles published in The Australian, The Conversation, The Daily Telegraph, The Herald Sun and the ABC Drum online.

His message is simple: Aboriginal affairs is everyone's business, Aboriginal people are not the victims of racism and colonisation, but rather, they are the victims of political correctness (a focus on differences and identity politics). His writings can be found at www. anthonydillon.com.au

Chapter Ten

WHY THERE IS CAUSE FOR OPTIMISM

It (society) is a partnership in all science; a partnership in all art; a partnership in all virtue, and in all perfection. As the ends of such partnership cannot be obtained in many generations, it becomes a partnership not only between those who are living, but between those who are living, those who are dead, and those who are to be born.
Edmund Burke, 1729-1797

This chapter asks the reader to consider the proposition that optimism is key to inter-generational cooperation and reward. It is a constant feature of the human desire not simply to survive, but to thrive. Of all the lessons of history, it is one our children deserve to learn.

There is great optimism in Irish-born parliamentarian and philosopher Edmund Burke's abovementioned notion of a "partnership" across the generations. A liberal thinker for his time, he is now thought of as the father of modern political conservativism. That approach means examining what has been left to us, preserving what can be shown to be of value, and improving on past practice when the case is made for change.

Burke's Ireland was strictly and harshly divided into a tiny number of elites ruling over a vast number of have-nots, with ultimate authority based in the English monarchy. An advocate of economic liberalism, limited government, and adherence to moral virtues in the interest of the public good, during his student years Burke founded a debating club at Trinity College Dublin. That club – renamed the College Historical Society (and nicknamed The Hist) celebrated its 250th anniversary in 2019. The then pro-Chancellor, Sir Donnell Deeney, emphasised that "the Hist has been at the forefront of major debates in Irish political, social and cultural life for the past 250 years … now more than ever before, discourse and debate are crucial in a democratic society and must be preserved and celebrated".

Many Australians are descendants of the illiterate poor of Burke's Ireland. Today, amid great concerns about the quality of Australian schooling – especially in English literacy – they might look to the rise of the Celtic Tiger as cause for optimism.

In 2024, based on data from the Program of International Student Assessment (PISA), Ireland ranked third among European countries for the quality of, and access to, education. Irish students achieved the highest average score in reading among the top 15 countries.

The Irish Republic has flourished, becoming a world leader in information technology and financial services as well as being recognised as the source of artistic, musical and literary giants. A few from that extremely long list include Oscar Wilde, George Bernard Shaw, Jonathan Swift, Bram Stoker, Edna O'Brien, James Joyce, Iris Murdoch, C.S. Lewis, Enya, U2 and Sinead O'Connor. According to the 2023 Better Life Index, Ireland outperforms the OECD average in jobs, education, health, social connections, safety and life satisfaction.

It is said that the purpose of education is to change a narrow mind into an open mind. Logically, a deliberate search for reasons to be optimistic indicates openness to new ways of looking at the world. The greatest cause for optimism is arguably found in the life and work of those who steadfastly – and often bravely – encourage and lead respectful debate. The well-informed exchange of ideas is essential to human progress.

Yet the same optimism and openness that distinguish the welcoming traditions of the West have rendered it vulnerable to anti-democratic and anti-intellectual agendas. Totalitarian regimes in Asia, Europe and the Middle East pose a deadly, daily threat to the West's ideals and the lives of all who support them.

Divisive narratives about Western racism, colonialism, sexism, classism and endless other *ism* grievances have taken hold. In what is described by some as the era of the "perpetually offended", there is little incentive or tolerance for genuine debate.

Its precious role in the evolution of Western civilisation has come under threat. American social psychologist Jonathan Haidt has called out the "safetyism" approach in education, whereby students are protected from potential emotional harms through the use of trigger warnings and safe spaces. During a visit to Australia in 2019, Haidt specifically warned against the stifling of debate in universities, saying the purpose of education is to make people think, not feel comfortable.

Notwithstanding scepticism about the command of language and portfolios displayed by generations of politicians, debating remains one of the great traditions on which Australia's parliamentary decision-making process continues to rely. As the House of Representatives Practice (7th Edition) explains:

> The effectiveness of the debating process in Parliament has been seen as very much dependent on the principle of freedom of speech. Freedom of speech in the Parliament is guaranteed by the Constitution, and derives ultimately from the United Kingdom Bill of Rights of 1688. The privilege of freedom of speech was won by the British Parliament only after a long struggle to gain freedom of action from all influence of the Crown, courts of law and Government.

Nelson Mandela, lawyer, civil rights activist and South Africa's first democratically elected President, was unequivocal about the importance of this skill when he explained that:

> A good leader can engage in a debate frankly and thoroughly, knowing that at the end he and the other side must be closer, and thus emerge stronger. You don't have that idea when you are arrogant, superficial and uninformed.

From the ancient Greeks through to Burke and beyond, debating remains one of the enduring traditions in the education of the young. Calls for a return to civil debate across the Western world are heartening.

According to the Australian Debating Federation, about 30,000

Australian students participate in debating competitions each year. The ADF says that,

> *Debating training imparts lifelong skills to students, including confidence in speaking in public to peers, an ability to logically make and assess arguments, and a willingness to engage with, and learn from, those with different opinions.*

These students, and their coaches and supporters, are cause for optimism. A renewed emphasis on debating – in all subjects across the school curriculum – would be a practical boost for young learners and for the nation.

Doing one's intellectual homework, thinking through the issues, and coming to a reasoned position on important topics are essential strategies for tackling the century's challenges. For better and for worse, Australians know that much of what originates elsewhere on the planet eventually makes it way here. This is globalisation, with all of its implications for politics, nationhood and international relationships, trade, socio-cultural and economic shifts, health, education, and myriad other issues.

Australians have a well-deserved reputation for optimism and curiosity about the world, for enjoying travel and adventure, and for accepting people at face value.

In this era of intense interest in environmental issues, for example, Australians are taking on responsibilities as custodians of nature, dedicated to conserving landscapes, resources and life forms. This comes from a belief that a heightened awareness of fragile ecosystems and the impact of human activity can mean the difference between species extinction and nature flourishing.

In the arts, there is cause for optimism, with record-breaking attendance at Australian museums and galleries in the post-Covid-19 years.

Similarly, every generation of Australians produces people with a passion for protecting mankind's noblest ideas, practices and achievements against loss and damage, particularly as these have been introduced, nurtured and defended here.

A record-breaking crowd attended the 2024 ANZAC Day service at the Australian War Memorial, with Air Vice Marshal Glen Braz emphasising that:

> Australians who found within themselves the selflessness and courage to serve our country, to serve you and protect our way of life … to these remarkable individuals, we say thank you.

Cause for optimism is also found in the words of Northern Territory Senator Jacinta Price, whose thoughtful embrace of her Indigenous and Anglo-Celtic ancestry includes reflections about the human settlement of this island nation. She says, "Our Australian story is not perfect. There are shameful chapters. But the arc of our history has been overwhelmingly positive. It's a story that has few historical parallels".

Sitting at the heart of the freest and wealthiest nations in history, the Judaeo-Christian tradition arguably offers the most optimistic world view of all. That optimism is reflected in centuries of growing commitment to individualism rather than statism, freedom of speech and assembly rather than authoritarian rule, and the rule of law rather than arbitrary punishment. Notwithstanding the scepticism around Christianity and other religions, all citizens deserve to understand that the pull factors that continue to attract hundreds of thousands of immigrants to Australia every year are unequivocally grounded in ancient Biblical concepts such as faith, justice, hope and charity.

Just before Christmas in 2021, following a second turbulent year of government responses to the COVID-19 pandemic, Australian author Luke Slattery pondered contemporary scientific evidence that "the human brain is hardwired towards supernatural beliefs." Slattery wrote that "A theme within mainstream Christianity that is often overlooked, if it hasn't been entirely forgotten, is optimism. A powerful belief in *human* potential and dignity emerged from the Italian Renaissance".

From cave to gulag to international conflict – through the darkest, coldest and most brutal times – individuals and societies have somehow found cause for optimism that has enabled them to persevere into the light of better days.

For centuries, deep thinkers and great writers have explored the best and the worst of human behaviour. Aleksandr Solzhenitsyn's extraordinary work, *The Gulag Archipelago*, for example, exposed the terror tactics of the Russian secret police and the labor camps which – particularly under socialist dictator Joseph Stalin – took the lives of millions of citizens. As a consequence, reinforced over and over again by evidence of the horrific treatment of dissenters, ideological supporters of anti-democratic regimes are challenged to think again.

If each generation is a bridge between those who have gone before and those to come, then the education of the young must include careful study of the triumph of the human spirit, magnificently represented in the enduring works of Western science, literature and the arts. These teachings are a gift for every age.

Australia's cultural legacy comprises three distinct parts: Western, Indigenous and immigrant.

Emma McCaul, this country's 2019 Thawley Essay prize winner and author of 'As history fades into history', points to the great irony that "Indigenous Australians know that history and culture must be fought for and proudly expressed if it is to be preserved and passed on to their children, but other Australians seem to have lost the will to take this path".

How many children still learn about author and disability rights activist Helen Keller (1880 – 1968)? Before the age of two, she lost her hearing and sight from illness. She wrote passionately about the optimism of researchers who believed they could teach the blind to read. She called Shakespeare "the prince of optimists" whose plays were about "looking forward to something better". She believed "the highest thinkers of the ages, the seers of the tribes and the nations, have been optimists".

Education is one of the best examples of the Australian tendency to pick up any shiny new idea that washes up on our shores and throw it into the mix in the hope that it will be transformative and take the focus off failed strategies that shone so brightly just a little earlier.

However, after decades of adopting experimental approaches with dire consequences for generations of students and teachers (especially in English literacy), Australian education might be among the first public policy areas to see a return to common sense.

Such is the current level of discontent among parents, employers and other stakeholders that authorities have seemingly had no choice but to rehabilitate and recast 'old school' approaches to curriculum, teaching and assessment.

Who knew, for example, that the acquisition of knowledge was so important, that a 'knowledge-rich curriculum' should be clear and easy to understand (especially for teachers!), and that academic progress generally comes from a 'sequenced' approach to teaching, learning and assessment?

Revelations about the 'science of learning' underpin the reforms. These are being promoted by national bodies such as the Australian Education Research Organisation (AERO) and by state education authorities such as the New South Wales Education Standards Authority (NESA) and South Australia's Department for Education.

Although much of the work is being led by the same people who have overseen decades of falling outcomes, their advocacy of so-called 'evidence-based' approaches may yet bring meaningful intellectual and academic improvements. Given the extraordinary power of human curiosity, and the dedication of teachers and school leaders, rethinking education in this way might lead to a rediscovery of wisdom, knowledge and skills from the past. If the proposals mean that young Australians will have access to more nationally consistent, intellectually rigorous, morally grounded and spiritually enriching education, that is cause for optimism. It makes it just possible that the bar will rise for all. The potential benefits for Australian society are endless.

To draw on Edmund Burke once again, it would help to think in terms of an inter-generational "partnership", whereby what has been proven to be sound is restored and what needs to change is reformed on the basis of knowledge and thoughtful debate.

Importantly, there is cause for optimism in the growing acknowledgement that artificial intelligence (AI) is not the magic solution. Wise heads remind us that learning must be intellectually challenging in order to bring real rewards.

Already, parents, communities and philanthropists around Australia are campaigning for smarter policymaking, because they are making conscious comparisons between what has been, what is, and what could be.

Operating quietly and determinedly in schools across this country are people who believe in teaching about character strengths, virtues and what Jonathan Haidt calls "the conditions that lead to high levels of happiness or civic engagement".

For example, optimism is key to the work of Australia's Positive Education Schools Association (PESA), the peak body whose vision is "for the science of wellbeing and Positive Psychology to be integrated throughout the education system, enabling all students, schools and communities to flourish". Examples of the longstanding success of this whole-school approach include Melbourne's Geelong Grammar and Ravenswood in Sydney. PESA's patron, Dr Martin Seligman, maintains that learning takes place when people's highest strengths are matched with their highest challenges. Schools "should teach both the traditional skills for academic attainment, and the skills needed to lead a flourishing life".

Australia's growing classical education movement places human virtues at the heart of curriculum and teaching. Echoing the work of thinkers across millennia – Socrates, Plato, Aristotle – this approach refocuses on the profound question, *what does it mean to live one's best life?* New schools are opening up each year, supported by Australian benefactors who want to see alternatives to mainstream providers.

Interestingly, between 2019 and 2023, all Australian states and territories saw a significant increase in home schooling, with over 40,000 students now being educated outside mainstream education systems. This is both an unfortunate statement of dissatisfaction with current offerings and an expression of the determination of Australian families to find better solutions. In a free and democratic society, it is a clear call for accountability and action.

In this third decade of the 21st century, following multiple indefensible government responses to the COVID-19 pandemic, reports of mental illness (especially among teenagers) have reached unprecedented levels. Analysts are highlighting the human costs of government-mandated isolation and uncertainty, inevitably resulting in the loss of personal and national optimism.

Digital technology wraps itself ever more intrusively around us, an unprecedentedly powerful force for both good and evil, and one for which the young, in particular, have been found to be unprepared.

Today's communication networks are so fast and so invasive that, as Winston Churchill apparently commented, "A lie gets halfway around the world before the truth has a chance to get its pants on".

Haidt's 2024 book, *The Anxious Generation*, describes the devastating effects of smart phones and social media on young people's mental health (particularly in the 15-24 age group). His research has resonated strongly with Australian parents and educators, and multiple studies have revealed the devastating consequences of pornography, sexting, gaming, bullying, violence and other online content. In this country, the revelations have led to some (often very belated) attempts by education authorities and individual schools to limit and even ban access to mobile devices during school hours.

But technology is arguably both the problem and the solution. An optimistic message should spread at the same speed as any other. The difference rests with the messenger.

Since 2020, the British writer JK Rowling – creator of *Harry Potter* – has given cause for optimism in taking a profoundly principled position on biologically determined sex differences in humans.

Rowling, who trained as an English teacher, is one of the high-profile individuals whose personal integrity and moral courage have been tested in the public square. For example, she has written that "the 'inclusive' language that calls female people 'menstruators' and 'people with vulvas' strikes many women as dehumanising and demeaning". She has questioned the medical and psychological consequences of gender reassignment, which has led to accusations of transphobia.

Her comments include the statement that "erasing the concept of sex removes the ability of many to meaningfully discuss their lives. It isn't hate to speak the truth". Like tennis legend Martina Navratilova and former Olympic gold medallist Caitlin Jenner, she rejects the entry of transgender athletes into women's sport.

Public figures, many of them parents, are essential defenders of freedom and personal responsibility. In the online world, in particular, their capacity to push back on illogical and counter-productive ideological movements is cause for optimism.

At the forefront of such efforts is Canadian psychologist Jordan Peterson, a high-profile role model for millions around the world because of his public presentations, podcasts and books such as *12 Rules for Life*. In 2023, Dr Peterson and former Australian Deputy Prime Minister John Anderson co-founded the Alliance for Responsible Citizenship (ARC), with the intention to lead "an alternative vision of the future" and "counter the pessimistic and apocalyptic narratives that seem to dominate the public landscape".

Every thinker, speaker, writer, artist, scientist who genuinely wants to contribute to the public and is not afraid to challenge the zeitgeist offers cause for optimism.

While technology provides platforms for aggression and intolerance, it also enables journalists, independent researchers, bloggers and vloggers, think tanks and publishers of all kinds to model the robust exchange of ideas in the service of a civil society. Australia has its fair share.

The list of public intellectuals committed to Western ideals is reassuringly long. Many have spent time in Australia or have influenced domestic debate. At over 90 years of age, American economist Thomas Sowell remains a source of erudition and wisdom. Others inspire variously with their curiosity, language, experience, youth and wit. Somehow, they resist the trolls, and despite accusations of being 'far right' Douglas Murray, Konstantin Kisin, Ben Shapiro and Joe Rogan bring candour and common sense to much-needed, long form discussions and debates. British philosopher Roger Scruton, who died in 2020, still influences with his ruminations on what is needed "if we are to live to our best ability".

In Australia, Josh Szeps' *Uncomfortable Conversations* and John Anderson's *Podcasts* stand out. While different in style, both explore critical issues at length and with a wide range of interviewees. Australia could do with many more like them.

Millennial Spencer Klavan, Yale graduate and lecturer in Greek at the University of Oxford, hosts a blog called the Young Heretics. He is a classical education devotee. Interviewed for his book, *Applying the Wisdom of the West to Modern Crises*, Klavan asserted:

> *It depends on reaching back into precisely this long tradition that we understand ourselves to be a part of, reaching into the wisdom of the past, asking how we might embody it in the here and now, and trusting that, in the long view of history, that effort will not be poorly spent; it will be well spent. In fact, the best thing that we can do, and the only thing really that we can do, whether things go well or badly, our job is basically the same, and that's to carry this light.*

An optimist looks for opportunities rather than seeing barriers; think of that 1980s word 'workaround' accompanying the rise of software technology. Optimism also reflects a more nuanced capacity to rationalise the good and bad things that happen in life. In this sense, optimism might be regarded as an evolved version of hope. Consider, for example, the difference between *I hope there is light at the end of the tunnel,* and *I am optimistic that there is light at the end of the tunnel.*

But there is evidence that Australians may be reaching a tipping point regarding trust in governments and other authorities.

According to statistics published by the Australian Department of the Treasury (2023), the proportion of citizens aged 15 and over who have "confidence in the national government" fell from 53.2% to 49.9% between 2006 and 2022. This matters, says the Treasury department, because "trust in government is linked to political participation, social cohesion and collaboration in tackling societal challenges". Closely connected to this are the findings of the annual surveys of Trust in

Australian Public Services. According to the Department of Prime Minister and Cabinet, the 2023 results showed that 61% of Australians reported that they trust public services, with three in four satisfied with the services.

In contrast, the Edelman Trust Barometer has found Australians to be deeply sceptical of government, business leaders, non-government organisations and the media. In 2024, the level of trust in government dropped to 45%. This followed a 2023 finding that 54% of Australians think "the nation's social fabric has become too weak to serve as a foundation for unity and common purpose". In 2022, a majority (61%) believed that it was impossible to have "constructive and civil debates about issues they disagree on – a foundational trait of a functioning and productive society, especially in democratic nations".

Mirroring these findings, surveys by McKinsey & Company and Rabobank Australia have identified a decline in optimism, a depressing finding in a nation once well known for its positive outlook.

This nation's character has long been seen as politically complacent, with a 'she'll be right' and 'no worries, mate' attitude somehow underpinning precious social cohesion and economic prosperity. While it may seem counter-intuitive, Australians' growing scepticism of governments and other decision-making bodies may also be the greatest cause for optimism. In 2023, against many predictions, Australians voted down a referendum proposal to make race-based changes to the Constitution, unconvinced by claims that this would improve the lives of Indigenous Australians. Instead, there have been widespread calls for more attention to be paid to the quality of policymaking and the ways in which billions of taxpayer dollars are spent.

Finding cause for optimism is important for individuals and for society at large. It is the key to establishing the "partnership" that lays the groundwork for successive generations.

Just as well-informed sceptics have always been needed to call out policy and leadership failure, improvements are arguably much more likely to be delivered by optimists.

Fiona Mueller was born in Darwin and is a longstanding resident of regional Australia who has also lived in Europe, the Middle East, Asia and the United States. A teacher of English and foreign languages, she worked in government and non-government schools in Australia and overseas before completing a doctorate, teaching at two universities and moving into state and federal education policy roles. Fiona's extensive practical experience led to her appointment as Head of ANU College at the Australian National University and then Director of Curriculum at the Australian Curriculum, Assessment and Reporting Authority (ACARA) in Sydney. Fiona is an Adjunct Fellow at the Centre for Independent Studies (Sydney) and a Senior Fellow of Advance HE (formerly the Higher Education Academy) in York, UK. In 2019, the Australian Financial Review's Power Issue placed her among the top five most influential people in education. In April 2022, she was appointed to a three-year term on the Australian Curriculum, Assessment and Reporting Authority (ACARA) Board as the nominee of the Commonwealth Government.